Feb/03   Lev

magical spells
for your home

magical spells
for your home

How to Bring Magic into Every
Area of Your Life

Ann-Marie Gallagher

BARRON'S

First published in the United States and Canada in 2002 by
Barron's Educational Series, Inc.

First published in Great Britain by Collins & Brown Limited
64 Brewery Road, London N7 9NT

A member of **Chrysalis** Books plc

All inquiries should be addressed to:
Barron's Educational Series, Inc.
250 Wireless Boulevard
Hauppauge, New York 11788
http://www.barronseduc.com

International Book Standard No.: 0-7641-5516-4

Library of Congress Catalog Card No.: 2001095274

Color reproduction by Classic Scan, Singapore
Printed by Craft Print International Limited, Singapore

987654321

Contents

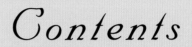

Introduction
The magic of the home

This is a book of spells based on the different rooms in your home, their associations, and their uses. It is also a guide to bringing magic into different areas of your life. So, you may well ask, how are the two connected? The answer is possibly more straightforward than you may realize. It is this: the home is more to us than simply shelter. At the most mundane level, it can also be a status symbol, with our income, taste, and level of acquisition speaking volumes about our status. At a slightly more subtle level, it is where we can put our feet up, both physically and psychologically. And at the level with which this book is concerned, it represents our security, our rootedness in the world, and our sanctuary from it. The different spaces in our home also symbolize different aspects of our lives, and you will find this reflected in the spells contained between the covers of this book.

Our homes, ourselves

The space in which we live, however humble or sophisticated, is therefore very important to us. It represents something of ourselves at a deeply rooted level. So when we dream of rooms in a house, we are often subconsciously sorting through different aspects of our lives: whatever lives in the basement may represent our deepest fears (and sometimes our desires), while the attic may contain memories as well as visions of the future. If our dream home is haunted, this is usually a sign that something is happening in our lives that needs exorcizing. This may sound very literal and clichéd, but sometimes dreams are!

In a similar way, this book uses different aspects of our everyday home to represent certain elements of our lives, each closely associated with the function of a room. For example, you will find spells for love, joyful relationships, fertility, and happy dreams in the chapter on the bedroom (see pages 82–101), while spells for clearing away bad habits, or for washing the blues away, are found in the chapter on the bathroom (see pages 102–111). The principle is simple: different rooms are put to specific uses, and often reflect particular aspects of our lives. *Magical Spells for your Home* links these rooms with the appropriate elements of our lives and offers spells connected with them.

Shared homes

You do not necessarily have to live in a house that contains all of the rooms mentioned in this book; most of the spells are relevant to everyday life whether you live in a mansion or share a small apartment. Wherever you live, you doubtless divide even very limited space into different uses, and these will still reflect (in the same way this book does) various facets of your life.

Your main problem, if you live in a one-room apartment or share an apartment or house with roommates, will be getting enough privacy to cast the spells and to leave some items undisturbed. Fortunately, the spells in this book are very practical in nature and often use everyday items found in the home, so you may get away with doing some of the spells and leaving a few objects hanging around without attracting attention! Today, alternative spiritual practices tend to be accepted as part of the pursuit for health and well-being, so you could pass off any chanting involved in your spellwork as an aid to meditation.

Magical housework

This is also a spellbook for the home in a more straightforward sense. It provides spells to promote a happy, healthy, and communicative environment—one in which household members can rest, restore their energy, socialize, shed stress, and feel protected. It contains a charm to hang in the hallway to bring good news to the door, and a spell to defend the home against ill wishers, as well as magical recipes to work on the energies within the home. These last are seen as particularly significant: if the space we inhabit is vital for our well-being, then it is important that the atmosphere in different areas of the home is appropriate to our relaxation, enjoyment, rest, or development.

Energy

The spells and advice offered in this book are designed to help you create the type of energy you need within your home space. The term "energy" has been batted about so much by "New Agers" that it has come to mean something rather nebulous and ill defined. Here, the word "energies" refers simply to the sort of feelings that you may experience when you step into a particular space, rather than to anything more arcane. In magic, intuition and emotion are taken seriously, as they are often key to sensing and understanding why we feel uneasy or discomfited without obvious reason. If there are spaces in your house that feel "cold" or uncomfortable without apparent cause, or you have ever walked into a room after an argument and felt as though you could "cut the atmosphere with a knife," as the saying goes, you will know what I mean. This doesn't mean that a room is haunted or that it houses an evil entity, simply that a bad atmosphere has built up that you are sensitive enough to detect. Using the spells provided will aid in clearing away such feelings and promoting a pleasant, protected atmosphere for the whole household.

Magic and personal problems

Ideally, our home is the place in which we can be ourselves without judgment, or the need to pretend we are other than we really are. When, sadly, this is not the case, we suffer because we do not have a space in which we can take shelter from outside problems and can rest and develop in a nurturing environment. Our relationship with our home is so close that our home life will be reflected in all aspects of our existence, and vice versa. This means that we can all suffer problems from time to time, and this spellbook recognizes this.

Magical Spells for your Home takes a realistic view; it does not claim that magic cures all ills, but rather encourages you to take practical steps to resolve problems. Whatever action you take, you will find that the spells provided can help you in a supportive and positively affirmative way, in conjunction with whatever practical steps you decide on.

How magic works

As I have indicated, the spells in this book are extremely practical, and many use everyday items already found in the home. However, if you have never cast a spell or used magic in this way before, you may be curious to know how magic works.

If you asked a hundred witches or magicians this question, you would probably get a hundred different answers. The magic described in this book is based on an old tradition, found all over the world: the custom of representing the things you wish to attain with objects, and of acting upon them to bring this about in reality. For example, the Lucky Bag spell (see pages 16–17) uses a drawstring bag to contain a nutmeg, a coin, a rosebud, and a sprig of rosemary. These objects represent good health, wealth, happiness, and protection respectively, being the attributes that the spell caster wishes to hold in their home. The person casting the spell uses these symbols to transmit a signal on the magical wavelength, which translates into change in the everyday level of reality known as the real world. This type of magic is known as "sympathetic magic."

The elements

The system of symbolism used to represent "like with like" in this book is based on several principles, most of which are native to the Western, developed world. The first of these is the elements, of which there are five in magic: Earth, Water, Fire, Air, and Spirit (the first four are most often referred to in the spells). Each of these elements corresponds with areas of human experience: Earth with wealth, fertility, and material matters; Water with the emotions, healing, and balance; Fire with willpower, and courage; Air with thought, memory, and communication.

Planetary influences

Complementing this system is the association of the days of the week with different planetary influences. Monday is the day of the Moon, Tuesday is associated with Mars, Wednesday with Mercury, Thursday with Jupiter, Friday with Venus, Saturday with Saturn, and Sunday, of course, is associated with the Sun. The planets themselves have correspondences with various aspects of human life:

- The Moon rules dreams, our psychological selves, and the human reproductive cycle.
- Mars is the patron of courage, the will, and has fiery characteristics.
- Mercury, messenger of the gods, rules communication, examinations, commerce, and transactions.
- Jupiter, the largest planet in our solar system, is expansive, generous, and the patron of fortune.
- Venus is the planet of love, harmony, sensuality, and beauty.

- Saturn, the ringed planet, stands for discipline, restriction, banishing, and repelling.
- And the Sun represents health and shines favorably on all aspects of our happiness.

Cycles of the Moon

You will notice that advice about the correct moon phase in which to carry out magical work is given for each spell. This is important: in magic, the Moon, our closest heavenly neighbor, is seen as an integral part of magic's tides. Just as it is observed to affect animal and plant life, and the movements of the seas and oceans, so the Moon is thought to affect humans too, and to steer the tides of magic. The magical community also uses it symbolically, as a part of the "sympathetic" system: a growing moon attracts and increases, whereas a waning moon repels and decreases. If you are not familiar with moon phases, they are easy to work out:

- A moon increasing from the right is a waxing (growing) moon, whereas a moon with the rounded edge on the left is a waning (shrinking) one. (See page 124.)
- The cycle is roughly 28½ days, with seven days from the New Moon (also known as the Dark Moon, when there is no moon visible in the sky) to the "first quarter," or waxing half-moon, then another seven days to the Full Moon.

◆ It is then seven days from the Full Moon to the "last quarter," or waning half-moon, then another seven days until the New Moon again.

It takes a little practice to connect with which moon phase you are in, and to calculate when you can cast spells. In the meantime, you can always use an ephemeris, which charts the Moon's cycle by the dates of the calendar, or consult a diary or daily newspaper that offers such guidance.

The source of tradition

In conjunction with the systems of the elements, planets, and timing, this book draws on the rich and varied magical and spiritual traditions of Western Europe. This includes stories, legends, and religious practices associated with ancient gods and goddesses; herbal knowledge; the secrets of the runes; and the metaphors that we find in the English language, which is itself an amalgamation of many languages, both ancient and modern. It includes a working knowledge of ancient and contemporary magical traditions, and applies the best of ancient customs and knowledge to modern-day life. Given that folk magic and herbalism were once part of everyday life in the home, *Magical Spells for your Home* can be said to be a continuing part of that rich tradition.

Practical magic

There may be terms and practices used within this book that are unfamiliar to some readers, or questions that you may have relating to practical issues, such as disposing of candles or other objects when you have finished with them. Here are some brief notes that should help you on your way:

Visualization

When you are asked to "visualize" something, this simply means creating a vision in your mind's eye: using your imagination.

Visualization can direct and increase the energy being poured into your spell. Practicing through meditation and using "visualization" tapes, whereby you work through a story in your imagination, can help considerably to develop this ability, as can frequent practice.

Circles

Sometimes you are asked to visualize a circle all around your working space; this does not occur in every spell, but where it does it is intended to help focus your energy and cut off outside distractions, thus aiding your concentration. These "circles" dissipate naturally at the end of a spell, so there is no need to "undo" them, unless you have particularly strong feelings that you should.

Directing energy

Some spells require you to send the energy you have raised into an object you are using; this simply requires concentration and practice. These spells offer more specific advice on how to direct your energy, and from where. Although this book contains all the advice that a beginner needs, you can develop this ability by finding out about energy points in your body, practicing "sensing" them, and working them out for yourself. If you get stuck, some yoga books provide helpful descriptions of exercises to develop awareness of your energy points.

Candles

As a rule, and unless advised otherwise, all candles should be allowed to burn down completely, safely, and under supervision at the end of spell casting.

Essential oils

The standard warnings apply to spells that use essential oils: pregnant women, those with high blood pressure and other sensitive conditions should avoid using them. These warnings are for your safety and should be observed. You will find a warning symbol in the "What you need" box for every spell that uses essential oils.

Leaving spells undisturbed

As a general rule, once items are buried or secreted, they should remain undisturbed, or should be treated as specifically directed in the instructions. The spell itself should also lie undisturbed, so don't talk about it and try to avoid "bothering" it by thinking about it too much. "Let it be" is the secret of successful spell casting!

Discretion

Once family, friends, or neighbors know you are using magic, you may have to face a number of reactions: some people are still very superstitious and view all magical activities as "evil"; some will be dismissive and will mock you; others may invest you with more power and wisdom than you actually have, and may demand remedies for all sorts of problems. Sometimes discretion is the best policy, so consider carefully your home situation and what makes sense in your own life, before revealing yourself to all and sundry as a budding magician.

Good luck to all who read and use the spells in this book. May they bring many blessings to you and your home!

Ann-Marie Gallagher
January 2002

Spell to bless your home

Creating a magical home

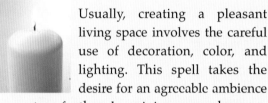

Usually, creating a pleasant living space involves the careful use of decoration, color, and lighting. This spell takes the desire for an agreeable ambience one step further by giving your home a spiritual "lift." It works by removing old, stale energies and replacing them with a fresh, new atmosphere. Whether it is used to bless a new abode or for psychic "spring cleaning" your present home, this spell is guaranteed to promote a healthy, nurturing environment.

The impulse to cleanse and bless the space in which we live has been with us since ancient times. For good luck, the Romans carried a flame from the hearth that they had left to the hearth they were going to, while the Celts were deeply superstitious about allowing a peat fire to die out. The ancient tradition of the "hearth fire" is continued in this spell, which calls upon the blessing of Vesta, Roman goddess of the hearth, and on the protection of Brighid, Celtic fire goddess, and culminates in the lighting of a candle to bless your home. The rosemary symbolizes cleansing, and is used here to sprinkle the salt water, a purifying mixture used in magic to clear away unwanted energies.

The spell can be carried out at any moon phase, and on any day of the week, as it both banishes old energies and welcomes in the new.

what you need...

Two white or cream household candles, approximately 6 inches/15 cm in length, placed in secure holders • Matches or a lighter • One bowl containing about 8 fluid ounces/250 ml of still spring water • One bowl containing one level teaspoon of ordinary salt • Four sprigs of fresh rosemary, tied in a bunch

what to do...

- Place all the ingredients in the center of the room where people are likely to congregate most frequently (usually the dining room or living room).
- Sit on the floor in the center of the room, and visualize a bright circle of light completely surrounding your home.
- Light one of the household candles.
- Lift up the bowl of water and say aloud:
  Water to heal and cleanse.
- Lift up the bowl of salt and say aloud: *Salt to purify and protect.*
- Pour the salt into the water, and stir it with the index finger of your writing hand until it has dissolved.
- Stand up and lift the salt water above your head, saying;
  Brighid,
  Goddess of the healing waters
  Of the flame that never falters

I drive out in your name
The spirits I no longer claim.

- Use the sprigs of rosemary to sprinkle the salt water around the floor and walls of every room. As you are "cleansing" each room in this way, open the windows and visualize the old atmosphere leaving through them, in the form of dark smoke.
- Close all windows and return to your "hearth" room.
- Take the other candle in both hands, and say aloud:
  Vesta,
  Goddess of the hearth
  Heart-fire of the path
  I bless in your name
  The home that I claim.
- Light the candle. You should ensure that there is a lit candle in this room whenever you use it after sunset.

Coming Home

Frontdoor spells

The entrance to your home is the site of many welcomes and farewells, and

the place where news and correspondence are customarily delivered. This

chapter provides spells to ensure good fortune, bring news, attract good vibes

and fend off bad ones, and help ensure the flow of energy through your home.

Each of these spells is intended to create a positive and happy environment.

Lucky Bag spell

Bringing good fortune

This spell uses a Lucky Bag—a collection of magical ingredients gathered together in a drawstring pouch—to contain all the luck you would wish for yourself and your home. The idea that you can "catch" and hold onto luck comes from a very long tradition. Corn dollies, for example, were originally woven to catch the spirit of the cornfield, so that it would return to bless the fields the next year. Likewise, the use of a pouch containing magical items dates back hundreds of years! The Lucky Bag should be purple—the color that symbolizes Jupiter, the planet of generosity and good fortune.

This spell requires a number of ingredients that symbolize luck in different areas of your life. They include a nutmeg for good health, a coin for wealth, a rosebud for happiness, and rosemary for protection. These four "lucks" are placed inside a satin drawstring bag, which is hung over your front door. As long as the Lucky Bag remains there, you will be assured of good fortune and of the four "lucks" contained within. If you move, take your Lucky Bag with you and cast the spell again, using fresh ingredients, to let the four "lucks" know where you now live.

Cast this spell on a waxing moon, to attract luck, and on a Thursday, the day of Jupiter.

what you need...

One purple candle, approximately 6 inches/15 cm in length, placed in a secure holder • One saucer of spring water • One saucer of salt • One small bunch of dried sage leaves • One fireproof dish • Matches or a lighter • One whole nutmeg • One highly polished coin, any denomination • One fresh rosebud, any color • One sprig of fresh rosemary • One purple satin drawstring bag, approximately 2 inches/5 cm square • Hammer • One 1 inch/2 cm masonry nail

what to do...

◆ Place all the ingredients in the room in which you will be working, with the candle, water, salt, and sage on the table.

◆ Visualize a circle of dazzling white light encompassing yourself and the table.

◆ Light the sage, blow out the flames, place in fireproof dish, and allow it to smolder.

◆ Light the candle, saying aloud:

Jupiter, ruler of fortune
Set my luck waxing with the Moon
Smile upon these fortunes four,
Let good luck enter through my door.

◆ Take the nutmeg and, holding it before the candle, say aloud: *This is the health of all who dwell here between turf and roof.*

◆ Pass the nutmeg through the sage smoke, saying:
I bless you by Air.

◆ Dip it in the salt, saying: *I bless you by Earth.*

◆ Dip it in the water, saying: *I bless you by Water.*

◆ Hold it above the candle flame, saying:
I bless you by Fire.

◆ Repeat this process with the coin, rosebud, and rosemary, naming them respectively as Wealth, Happiness, and Protection.

◆ When you have named the four "lucks," place them in the bag and tie it tightly, saying:

As I hold you and cherish you,
Cherish you and hold you me
By Jupiter, so mote it be.

◆ Carry the bag to your front door, envisaging as you do so the circle of light moving with you and shrinking, until it surrounds only the bag.

◆ Nail the bag to the wall above your front door and keep it there for as long as you live between the turf and the roof!

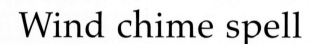

Wind chime spell

Bringing good news to your door

Folklore claims various reasons for the use of wind chimes in and around the home. They are believed to ward off evil spirits, attract fairies, or give the wind a voice! Here, they are used to honor the element of Air, which is the spirit of communication and the patron of messengers. This spell is particularly good for easing the flow of communication to and from your home, creating a tranquil atmosphere, and bringing good news to your door.

It uses the old wisdom that music and clatter alike drive away evil influences and attract good spirits. Because different noises provoke different reactions within each of us, you will need to find a set of wind chimes that sound harmonious to you. The feathers used in this spell symbolize birds, which were depicted in ancient times as messengers of the gods. Their appearance in temples and on statues was regarded as an omen of both good and bad fortune, and their flight patterns were studied in order to predict anything from the future of a newborn baby to the outcome of a battle.

This spell calls upon the powers of Athena, goddess of communication. It is best cast on a waxing moon, for positive energy flow, and on Wednesday, the day of Mercury, planet of communication.

what you need...

One tablespoon of water • Three drops of lavender essential oil • One oil burner with a tea light (or votive) • Matches or a lighter • One yellow candle, approximately 6 inches/15 cm in length, placed in a secure holder • Three x 8 inch/20 cm lengths of yellow ¼ inch/½ cm-wide ribbon • Three bird feathers, any color, gathered after they have been shed naturally • One set of wind chimes

what to do...

◆ Add the lavender oil and water to the burner, and light
it. Light the yellow candle, saying aloud:
Athena,
Goddess of communication,
Empower and bless my spell
To bring good news to my door
With the swiftness of a bird in flight,
Good fortune to ensure.

◆ Using a length of ribbon, tie the first of the bird
feathers onto any thread on the wind chime, chanting
as you do so:
Happy news, find your way
To my home, from today.

◆ Tie a second feather to another thread on the
wind chime, chanting:
Bright music, sacred sound
Evil here, never found.

◆ Tying a third feather to yet another thread on the
wind chime, chant:
Lucky breeze, happy din
Summon light, to flow in.

◆ Hang your enchanted wind chime in a porch, or
over your front door, where any breeze or movement
will stir it into action.

Mirror Spell

Welcoming good energies and defending against bad

In magic, mirrors are often used to reflect, bounce back, and intensify energy. This spell uses a double-sided mirror to reflect and bounce back ill intentions coming toward your house, and to intensify the good vibes inside it. Reflections and glass have long been associated with water, the element of balance, love and healing. These energies are welcome in any home, and as the inward-facing mirror meets the balance, love and healing generated by you, it will multiply it within the household. The outward-facing mirror, although intended to bounce back ill feelings to those sending them toward you, also restores balance, love, and healing in the lives of ill wishers once they are shown the error of their ways. When ill wishes are reflected back onto the sender, they are more likely to "see" how badly they are behaving.

Using mirror magic in this way is not a "curse"; what the sender experiences is neither more nor less than they have sent toward you. This is an ethical and fair way to deal with bad "vibes" that originate from the resentment of others. Remember, the mirror will also bounce back positive energy to those who perform good deeds. Cast this spell on a Dark (New) Moon, which is best for building protection, and on a Saturday, the day of Saturn, which is the planet of boundaries and teacher of discipline.

what you need...

One salt shaker with a flowhole • One black candle, approximately 6 inches/15 cm in length, placed in a secure holder • Matches or lighter • One charcoal disk • One fireproof container • One teaspoon of dried juniper berries • One double-sided round mirror, or two single-sided round mirrors of similar size (any), glued back to back

what to do...

- Take a bath (using half a teaspoon of salt) prior to casting this spell, and work naked or at least barefoot.
- Place all ingredients in the center of the space in which you will be working.
- Sitting in the center of your working space, visualize a series of rings like those of the planet Saturn, encircling the entire room.
- Light the black candle, saying aloud:

    Saturn, planet of restriction
    Guard my home from malediction
    Guide into the right direction
    All the good found in reflection
    To those seeking to attack
    Reflect the ill and send it back.

- Place the charcoal disk in the fireproof container, light it and when it glows red hot, sprinkle the juniper berries on it.
- Pass both sides of the mirror through the incense smoke, saying:

    Be purified.

- Place the mirror flat and pour salt onto it in the shape of an eye, saying:

    See all evil and turn it away
    Whatever others do or say.

- Turn the mirror over, allowing the salt to fall to the ground, and pour salt onto the reverse surface in the same way, saying:

    See all good and magnify, Within whatever you espy.

- Take the mirror to a window at the front of your house, and hang or stand it there, placing the surface that is to bounce back evil vibes facing outward, and the surface that is to magnify good energies facing inward.
- Your magical mirror should now be left undisturbed.

FRONTDOOR SPELLS

✳

Wind sock spell

Conducting the flow of energy through your home

Occasionally it is possible to detect an unsettled atmosphere in your home, or to get the feeling that things are somehow out of balance. This may lead you to conclude that your home has either hosted unpleasant events in the past or is haunted. However, nine times out of ten what is actually being experienced, at an emotional level, is a blockage of the normal energy flow. We humans tend to trail our feelings around with us, leaving imprints of our personal energy—our spiritual "signatures"—in the places we most frequent. If the natural rhythm gets blocked in some way, then pockets of excess energy (or even an energy vacuum) may be felt.

This is because the same ability that enables us to leave our imprint also makes some of us sensitive to either its absence or its presence.

The Chinese tradition of Feng Shui provides a system for positioning objects in the home to ensure the free flow of energy. This wind sock spell employs the European tradition of "sympathetic magic," using the Western symbolism of the five elements. Here, the elements of Air and Water work together to restore the flow of energy through your home. The wind sock is shaped like a fish: an ancient symbol of wisdom and unity with the elements. Cast this spell on a waxing half-moon to encourage balance, on a Monday in honor of the Moon, the ruler of psychic energy.

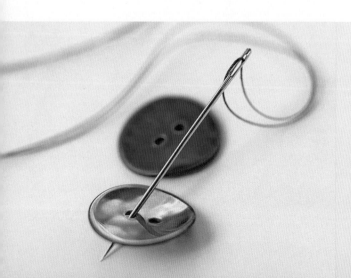

what you need...

One sandalwood incense stick, placed in a holder • One small bowl of spring water • One white candle, approximately 6 inches/15 cm in length, placed in a secure holder • Matches or a lighter • One 12 x 12 inch/30 x 30 cm square of material in any green • One 12 x 12 inch/30 x 30 cm square of material in a contrasting green • Standard sewing needle and green thread • Three 12 inch/30 cm lengths of fine wire • Two matching buttons, any size

what to do...

- Place all the ingredients in the center of the space in which you will be working.
- Sit in the center of your working space, placing the incense to your right and the water to your left.
- Visualize a circle of flowing light encircling the entire room.
- Light the incense and the candle in silence.
- Take one square of fabric, and stitch a ½ inch/1 cm hem on two opposite sides.
- Sew the two remaining sides together, to form a tube with a hem at each end, leaving a small gap through which to thread the wire.
- Thread two of the lengths of wire through the hems and shape the material into a tube, using the third wire

- to form a loop with one of the "mouths" of the tube, by which the wind sock fish will be hung up.
- From the remaining piece of fabric, cut out two side fins and a fish tail and sew these onto the tube in appropriate positions.
- Sew the buttons on to form eyes; these should be equally balanced on each side of the tube.
- Pass the finished wind sock through the incense smoke, sprinkle it with some of the water, and hold it before the candle for seven heartbeats.
- Hang your fish wind sock from the ceiling or beam, wherever you wish to facilitate the flow of energy in your home.

Resting and Relaxing

Living room spells

The living room is usually the space in which you relax or seek

entertainment, so it is particularly important that the atmosphere here is

conducive to both. The spells in this chapter aim to create tranquility and a

lighthearted atmosphere, fend off stress, help you re-energize, and protect

you from unpleasantness. Choose those that match the ambience you wish

to create for rest and relaxation.

Floating candle spell

Creating a space for rest and enjoyment

For the majority of us, the living room is a place to unwind and relax, whether we are watching television, listening to music or reading. Most of the time these functions are combined, but there may also be occasions when we wish to bring a little more tranquility into our lives by retiring to the living room to meditate or do relaxation exercises. This spell inspires an atmosphere that is conducive to both entertainment and relaxation, and has the added bonus of providing the room with an attractive centerpiece.

In magical traditions, the colors green and blue are used to symbolize the elements of Water and Earth. Here, Water is used to invoke peace and harmony, while Earth (the element of physicality and animal comforts) provides a sense of physical well-being. Psychologically, both colors are very easy on the eye, and produce a sense of rest and calm. The spectacle of flames on water concentrates the mind on both stillness and energy, and is uplifting.

This spell calls upon the goddess Rhiannon, a Welsh deity associated with the sea, and on Demeter, an ancient Greek earth goddess, to lend their energies to the enchantment. It is best carried out on a waxing or Full Moon, on any day of the week apart from Saturday, the day of restrictive Saturn.

what you need...

One blue candle, approximately 6 inches/15 cm in length, placed in a secure holder • Matches or a lighter • One green candle, approximately 6 inches/15 cm in length, placed in a secure holder • One large decorative glass bowl, half filled with water • Two blue floating candles • Two green floating candles

what to do...

- Put the ingredients on a low table in your living room.
- Visualize a web being woven at speed around the walls of the entire room.
- When the web cocoon is complete, light the blue candle, saying:
  Rhiannon,
  Lady of Tides,
  Let all who drift into this space
  Becalm themselves and slow their pace.
- Light the green candle, saying:
  Demeter,
  Ruler of growth,
  Let all who seek enjoyment here
  Be nurtured by the atmosphere.
- Place your hands, palms down, just above the water in the bowl, and visualize people sitting around the room, talking, joking, watching television, reading, and looking happy. Imagine the feeling that arises from that vision traveling through your body, down your arms, through your hands, and into the water.
- When you feel that you have "charged" the water and the bowl with the vision of enjoyment and rest, light the blue, then the green, floating candles, saying:
  Green is the color of the trees,
  And Nature's balm that brings us ease,
  Blue is the color that is best
  For soothing souls and bringing rest
  So may these candles bring good cheer
  By showing these are honored here
  So mote it be!
- Renew the green and blue floating candles, and the water, whenever you need to refresh the atmosphere of calm and enjoyment.

Grounding spell

Deflecting everyday stresses

Everyday modern life is full of stresses that have the potential to develop into serious strains on our health or our relationships. This is true whether you are a high-flying entrepreneur, a student, a secretary, a factory worker, or a full-time parent. It is especially important, therefore, that our living spaces provide us with a sense of "groundedness" against the stresses that cause instability and imbalance in our lives.

This spell literally "grounds" your stress, as it uses soil, or compost, in which you can symbolically bury your anxieties. It combines an old magical technique—that of letting the

element of Earth sort out the bad energies from the good and thus provide stability—with the modern magic of psychological "self-talk." This provides an ideal brew for those coping with modern life and its accompanying strains, and a beautiful visual feature for your living room. Whenever you water your plant, remember that you are not only nourishing the plant, but also growing the spell that keeps you grounded. This will add to the spell's power.

This spell should be carried out on a New Moon, as this is a good time to strengthen yourself from within. It can be done on any day of the week.

what you need...

Three sheets of old newspaper • One standard terra-cotta flowerpot, approximately 5 inches/13 cm in diameter • Bulb compost to fill the pot • One small gardening trowel or a dessertspoon • One black candle, approximately 6 inches/15 cm in length, placed in a secure holder • Matches or a lighter • One salt shaker • Ink pen with some black ink • One strip of paper approximately 1 x 4 inches/2.5 x 10 cm • One flowering bulb, any indoor variety

what to do...

- Place all the ingredients on a table in the center of the living room, with the sheets of newspaper underneath the pot.
- Half fill the flowerpot with compost, using the gardening trowel or spoon.
- Light the candle, saying:
  May the energies of the New Moon
  Who takes away unwanted things,
  And transforms them,
  Do the same for what I commit to this Earth.
- Using the salt shaker, create a circle of salt around the base of the pot, and not less than 3 inches/7.5 cm away from it.
- Take the pen and write down on the strip of paper the word "STRESS."
- Press the paper hard between your hands and imagine all the anxiety and pressure that you feel at the end of a difficult day passing into it.
- Roll the paper up into a tiny, tight scroll and push it into the compost in the pot.
- Place the bulb in the pot, and cover it with compost up to the end of the shoot.
- Place your palms on the soil in the pot, saying:
  Earth take away
  All I wish away
  Transform all gloom
  Into flowers that bloom.
- Take a deep breath and blow away the circle of salt.
- Care for your bulb in accordance with any instructions that come with it, and repeat the action with the pen and paper scroll whenever you feel the need to de-stress and get "grounded."

Fire rune spell

Transforming relaxation into energy

This spell helps you to maximize the benefits of a good, relaxing home life by turning it into energy whenever you feel the need. The old northern peoples of Scandinavia recognized the benefits of a stable home life: an ancient blessing for newly married couples wished "flag, flax, fodder and frig" for them, meaning hearth, clothing, food, and love. Happily, they have left us a legacy of their wisdom: an alphabet of "runes," magical symbols dating from pre-Christian times that were found scratched or carved onto stones. Combining the concept of the "hearthstone" with an appropriate rune symbol, this spell transforms the inner power generated by rest and nurtures it into a dynamic and fiery energy when you most need it.

Open fires are rare in modern homes, but because it is the spirit of the hearth (rather than its physical presence) that counts, you should find a place that you feel is the "heart" of your living room, ideally near a source of heat. The rune used here is known as "Eoh" (pronounced "Eeyer" and shown in the picture on page 31), which represents transformation. Appropriately for a spell that seeks swift change, Eoh resembles the zigzag shape made by lightning strikes. The best time for casting this spell is on a Sunday, the day of the Sun, and on a waxing moon, to attract energy.

what you need...

One sheet of old newspaper • One smooth, palm-sized stone, oval and slightly flattened • One small pot of black craft oil paint • One fine paintbrush • One red candle, approximately 6 inches/15 cm in length, placed in a secure holder • Matches or a lighter

what to do...

- Place all the ingredients on your "hearth," ensuring that the newspaper is positioned under the stone, paint, and brush.
- Light the candle, saying:
  I call upon the power of Fire
  To work itself to my desire,
  Take the lightning from the storm
  That energy shall be transformed
  And with the blessing of the rune
  It shall be mine within one moon.
- Paint the rune "Eoh" onto the center of one side of the stone. The rune should be approximately 1½ inches/4 cm high.
- Taking care not to smudge the wet paint, take the stone in both hands and, keeping your eyes on the symbol you have just painted, chant toward it no fewer than 30 times the name of the rune: Eoh.
- When you have done this, lift the stone above your head in both hands, saying:
  By my breath and by my mote
  By my blood and by my bones
  Witness, Fire, this mark and note
  The power held in this stone
  That whenever I need energy,
  As I will it, so shall it be.
- Place your hearthstone on your "hearth," and allow the candle to burn down safely next to it. Ensure that your "fire rune" stone is undisturbed for at least one moon cycle (a month).
- Thereafter, whenever you need to transform rest into energy, all you have to do is touch the stone, say the word "Eoh" aloud, and silently ask for the energy you need.

Feather spell

Lightening the atmosphere with laughter

Because it is a shared space, the living room is often where family discussions or exchanges take place, and these may sometimes be a little "heavy!" Sensitive souls can often detect an unhappy atmosphere after a family argument simply by walking into a room where people have been shouting or quietly fuming after disagreements. Although this can build up in any shared area of the house, it is particularly important to guard against this in the living room, because this is where we should most be able to enjoy rest and respite from stress. This spell is a great antidote to the "heavy weather" generated by the natural tensions of shared living space.

It hardly needs saying that feathers represent lightness, but they are also used here as symbols of laughter. This spell calls upon Baubo, the ancient Greek goddess of laughter. Wise old Baubo, so the legend goes, entertained Demeter, the Earth goddess, when she was mourning the disappearance of her daughter, the Spring goddess, Persephone. Baubo was clever enough to know that laughter helps us to forget our troubles when there is nothing we can do about them.

This enchantment is best woven on the waxing moon, to attract a good atmosphere, and on a Wednesday, the day of the planet Mercury who rules Air.

what you need...

Either the Fool card from a tarot deck or the Joker card from a standard deck of playing cards • One yellow candle, approximately 6 inches/15 cm in length, placed in a secure holder • Matches or a lighter • Three bird feathers, either white or gray, shed naturally • One 18 inch/45 cm length of narrow yellow ribbon

what to do...

- Place all the ingredients on the floor in the center of your living room, standing the Fool or Joker card up against the candle so that you can see it throughout the spell casting.
- Visualize a circle of pale silvery light completely encircling the room.
- Light the candle, saying:
  Old woman, Wise Fool,
  Baubo, it is you I call,
  Cast sadness from this place forever
  Make hearts within as light as feathers.
- Take the feathers in a bunch and fan them out from the stalks. Tie them in this position, winding the yellow ribbon around and between the stalks. As you do this, chant the following words:

From the floor
To the rafters
Lift the roof with
Sound of laughter.

- Fasten off the ribbon, and hold the feather "fan" in front of the card so that the Fool or Joker witnesses the completion of the spell.
- Place the card back in the pack, allow the candle to burn down safely, and position the fan, feathers upward, on a mantelpiece or shelf in the living room.

Matchstick spell

Protecting you from your enemies

There are times in all our lives when we feel in need of protection against the outside world, and against the ill will of others. The flip side of this is the need to feel positively supported, and this little bit of magic works on both principles. As well as guarding you from the "evil eye" of others' bad intentions, the matchstick figure created in this spell offers the blessings of the Sun to those in need of support. Thus it fends off ill feeling from outside the home, and nurtures the strength and support found within it. Of course, the spell will only work if you have truly not deserved the bad feelings of those who wish you harm.

The matchsticks used here are shaped in a St Andrew's cross arrangement. This X-shape has ancient origins, traditionally blocking entry and bringing love. The latter is seen in the way that we mark kisses on cards and letters—this is actually the symbol of the rune "Gifu," meaning "Gift," (and it is inscribed on the candle below). Rune wisdom tells us that Gifu signifies both the giving and receiving of gifts, and this spell should only be cast if there is a positive commitment to give and take in your relationships with friends and enemies alike.

The spell should be done on a full or half-moon, to reflect your intentions of defending and bringing, and can take place on any day of the week.

what you need...

One needle, any size • One tea light or votive • One matchbox with a lighting strip • Three long wooden matches • Ordinary matches or a lighter • One length of black cotton, exactly nine times the length of the index finger on your writing hand • Hammer • One small tack

what to do...

- Place all the ingredients in the center of your living room.
- Using the needle, inscribe an "X" into the surface of the tea light or votive.
- Light the tea light or votive with ordinary matches or a lighter.
- Visualize a double circle of light (with an inner and an outer ring) completely surrounding the room.
- Taking two of the long matches, with the heads upward, use the cotton to bind them into an X-shape, and continue winding the cotton around them until it has all been used up, leaving just enough cotton to tie a loop and fasten off.
- Hold the matchstick X at a safe height above the candle flame, saying:
  Fend off harm,
  Nurture love,
  As below,
  So above.
- Take the third long match, light it, and with its flame light the heads of the bound matches, saying: So mote it be! before immediately blowing them out.
- Hammer the tack to your living room window frame, and hang the matchstick X in your window, where it can be seen from both inside and outside, if possible.
- The next time you go out of the house, bring back in with you a gift to be shared among all who live there, be it a plant, a candle, fruit, or some choco-late—and enjoy!

Eating and Meeting

Dining room spells

Dining space is also a meeting area in many households, and the site where relationships between families and friends are conducted. This means that the dining room tends to see a lot of emotional traffic. This chapter dishes up spells for healing differences, improving communications, bringing company to your home, dealing with relatives, nurturing friendships, and keeping your neighbors sweet. Bon appétit!

DINING ROOM SPELLS

Salad spell

Mending quarrels in the home

Whether you share a home with friends or family, quarrels can be distressing for all concerned. Even in cases where it is obvious where the blame lies and easy to see the solution, the general unpleasantness of a disagreement can cast a shadow over the whole household. This spell works best where the occupants are accustomed to sharing meals together, because it will require all quarreling parties to participate in eating the results, as described below.

In life we are often required to swallow the bitter as well as the sweet, and in magic there are ways of symbolizing this. The various salad leaves used here are a mixture of bitter and sweet—or, at least, nutty flavors. Cucumber is added to cool tempers down. Herbs, such as the basil and mint, have been used in magic for thousands of years, and their medicinal effects are put to good use here. For example, basil helps to allay depression and impatience. The spell works its magic by mixing leaves and herbs together in a harmonious fusion of taste, thus symbolizing the restoration of balance between opposites. Where better to achieve this than in the dining room, the focus of gossip, news, banter, and of course eating?

Cast this spell on a waxing or waning half-moon to attain a truce, on any day of the week.

what you need...

One white and one black candle, approximately 6 inches/ 15 cm in length, placed in secure holders • Matches or a lighter • Equal amounts of these leaves: iceberg or lollo rosso, plain leaf or oak leaf, spiderleaf or wild rocket, and corn salad/lamb's leaf • Small bunch of fresh basil leaves • Small bunch of fresh mint leaves • 16 thin slices of cucumber • Honey and mustard dressing, made from wholegrain English mustard, honey, fresh lemon juice, virgin olive oil, and white-wine vinegar • One salad bowl

what to do...

- Place all the ingredients on the dining room table, with the white candle to your right and the black candle to your left.
- Light the candles.
- Visualize a circle of silver light encompassing yourself and the tables and chairs.
- Take the iceberg or lollo rosso and the plain leaf or oak leaf and place them in the salad bowl, saying:
  Bland-to-taste and bitter leaf
  Be you balanced in your grief.
- Take the spider leaf or wild rocket, and corn salad or lamb's leaf and place them in the bowl, saying:
  Peppered sweetness, flavor mild
  Blend to tame that which is wild.

- Throw in the basil and mint, saying:
  Basil sweet to lift the mind
  Mint enjoin all to be kind.
- Finally, add the slices of cucumber, saying:
  Coolness full grown in hot season
  Bring combatants to cool reason.
- Mix together the mustard, honey, lemon juice, olive oil, and vinegar to make the dressing, and add to the salad to freshen and bind it; then call everybody together to eat.
- When everyone has left the table, blow out the candles, but light them again at each subsequent meal until they have fully burned down.

DINING ROOM SPELLS

Speech bubbles spell

Promoting communication at the table

A lot of communication happens over food: a glance at the way that a family or group of room-mates behave when sharing a meal often tells you all you need to know about what is going on in that house-hold! Thankfully, it is less common nowadays to observe rules of "silence when eating," and for some people meals are the main time when family or house matters are discussed. Smooth communication in the dining room is, therefore, a matter of key importance in the general exchange of information, ideas, and interpersonal contact throughout the house. A little bit of magic to improve the flow of conversation is what this spell is all about.

In magic, Air is seen as the element of all forms of communication. It is thus associated because, physically, vibrations that travel through the air create sound, and of course we have to draw breath in order to speak. There is also a historical connection: the feathers used for quill pens in the past were derived from birds, whose home element is the Air. Air is used in this spell to produce bubbles, which carry your wishes, then burst, releasing the magic to do its work.

Try this spell on a Wednesday, the day of the communications planet Mercury, and on a waxing moon to increase the power of communication in the home.

what you need...

One yellow candle, approximately 6 inches/15 cm in length, placed in a secure holder • Matches or a lighter • One tablespoon of water • Three drops of pine essential oil • One oil burner with a tea light or votive • One bottle of soap bubbles, complete with a wand • Three sycamore "keys" (seeds) that have fallen naturally from the tree

what to do...

- Place all the ingredients in the center of the dining table.
- Light the candle, saying:
  Element of Air
  Bless all who gather here
  With bright conversation
  And the ability to listen.
- Place the water and essential oil in the bowl of the oil burner and light the tea light or votive.
- Open the bottle of soap bubbles and, moving clockwise (deosil or sunwise) around the room, create a circle of power by blowing bubbles through the wand all over the room.
- Take the sycamore keys and hold them above the oil burner, saying:
  Seeds that have traveled through the air
  Containing the knowledge of the trees
  Unlock the magic that is carried
  On the Air and in the breeze.
  Then place them in the bowl of the oil burner.
- Standing in the center of the room, close your eyes and picture in your mind's eye friends and family gathered around the dining table having enjoyable conversations.
- Taking a deep breath, blow showers of bubbles into the air three times, imagining those images into the bubbles.
- Put out the candle and allow the essential oil to scent the whole room.
- Burn the yellow candle a little at sundown on each subsequent day until the Full Moon, when you should allow it to burn down completely.

Cutlery spell

Bringing company to your home

If you have recently moved home, or have changed your situation in some way, your social diary may be emptier than usual. Of course, you could invite people to dinner or throw a party—but sometimes a little magic will generate a more spontaneous social flow. This spell ensures that friends and neighbors head toward your home, so be certain that you really want their company before you set about casting it!

The symbol made by the crossed knife and fork in this spell signifies that there is always a place reserved at your table for guests. It also represents an X as marked on a map—a destination—sending out a message onto the magical web that X marks the spot where treasure can be found. The riches that your guests will find at the end of the trail is, hopefully, hospitality and good company. You will need to keep standby quantities of tea, coffee, and cookies at the ready. The Fruit bowl spell (see pages 44–45), the Friendship cake spell (see pages 46–47), and the Honey sandwich spell (see pages 48–49) will come in very handy for times when relatives, friends, or neighbors come by, and you can double up on the quantities of some of the spells. Cast this spell on a Thursday, the day of expansive and hospitable Jupiter, and on a waxing moon, to attract company.

what you need...

One pink candle, approximately 6 inches/15 cm in length, placed in a secure holder • Matches or a lighter • One eggcup containing salt • One eggcup containing virgin olive oil • One eggcup containing water • One fresh, uncut loaf of bread • One dining knife and fork

what to do...

- Place all the ingredients in the center of the dining table.
- Visualize a circle of golden light surrounding the whole room.
- Light the candle, saying:
  Pink for affection
  Friendship and pleasure
  Bend your direction to
  Find what you treasure.
- Pour the salt onto the table, saying:
  May we season friendship with good conversation.
- Anoint the table with a little of the oil, saying:
  May your path to my table be smooth and swift.
- Sprinkle a little water onto the table, saying:
  May love and affection guide you, and a river of friends flow to my door.

- Break the loaf into three equal parts, saying:
  May we all eat heartily whenever we meet.
- In the center of your dining table cross the knife over the center of the fork, right to left, in an X-shape, saying:
  There is always a place at this table for guests
  From North and from South, from East and from West
  And those seeking company here will be blessed
  For all that is shared here is all that is best.
- Use one-third of the loaf for your household, and sprinkle the remaining two-thirds outside to the North, South, East, and West of your house, for the birds.

Fruit bowl spell

Coping with difficult relatives

There is an oft-quoted saying that we can choose our friends, but we can't choose our families. This old adage comes to the fore whenever we have difficulties with our relatives, because we are reminded that family relationships represent different types of commitment from those we have with friends and acquaintances. After all, an irretrievable falling out with a friend can lead you to decide to end the relationship so that you are no longer friends; a quarrel with your aunt doesn't stop her being your aunt. Family obligations often call for far more tact, particularly when relatives are unsympathetic to your lifestyle, or quarrelsome to start with!

This spell is guaranteed to mollify crabby aunts and curmudgeonly uncles alike, and ensure that, at least while they are in your house, sharp tongues will be sweetened and stilled. The various fruits and their colors symbolize a variety of qualities that you wish for in your troublesome relatives, but you will need to ensure that you cast this spell in advance of any visits from them. If they tend to just drop by uninvited, you could always deploy the Ringstone spell (see pages 120–121) to discourage them from doing so.

Cast this spell on a waxing moon, to promote cordial relationships, and on any day apart from Saturday, the day of restrictive Saturn.

what you need...

One empty fruit bowl • Two white candles, approximately 6 inches/15 cm in length, placed in secure holders • One bowl of spring water • One clean kitchen towel • Four sweet-variety red apples • Four sweet-variety oranges • Four sweet plums • One small bunch of red or green seedless sweet grapes • If available, a handful of cherries

what to do...

- Place the ingredients on your dining table, with the fruit bowl at the center and the candles on either side of it.
- Place the bowl of water and the kitchen towel side by side, with the fruit nearby.
- Visualize a circle of glowing red light encompassing the whole room.
- Light the right-hand candle first, saying:
  I honor my bloodline.
- Light the left-hand candle, saying:
  I honor decent behavior.
- Raise your writing hand above the water and say:
  This pure water carries my good intent
  Sharpness to sweeten, unkindness to prevent.
- Now wash the fruit in the spring water and dry it with the kitchen towel, piece by piece.
- First, take the apples and place them in the fruit bowl, saying:
  Fruit from my family tree
  Kindness bring and sweetness be.
- Then place the oranges in the fruit bowl, saying:
  Pip and pith, kith and kin
  Fruit and leaf bring goodness in.
- Next put in the plums, saying:
  Fruit and stone, flesh and bone
  Sweetness stays, sourness gone.
- Put in the grapes, saying:
  Other fruit on the vine,
  Stillness bring, peace be mine.
- If available, put in some cherries, saying:
  Root and branch, stalk and cherry
  Meetings here be brief and merry.
- Keep these fruits on the dining table whenever your troublesome relatives visit, and encourage them—if you can—to partake of them.

Friendship cake spell

Nurturing friendships

Those of us who dearly value our friendships realize how important it is to nourish them. It is easy for busy, but well-meaning people to lose contact with good friends: our hectic lives sometimes lead us to forget to nurture our friendships. Ironically, this usually happens precisely because good friends are generally the people who are most tolerant when we forget to call or are too distracted to keep up with them. This spell builds on the sentiment so often expressed when someone welcome drops by unexpectedly: "If I'd known you were coming, I would have baked a cake!" Here, you bake a delicious cake to let your friends know that you value them, and add some special magic to the recipe.

Making magic is often compared to baking: you decide what is needed, gather the ingredients, blend them according to the right method, then let time pass before it is ready. It isn't often that you get to eat the results, however, so this spell carries a bonus for sweet-toothed magicians! Bake this Friendship cake and invite your best buddies around for a wonderful afternoon tea.

This spell is best cast on a Friday, day of the friendship planet Venus, and on a waxing moon, for growth.

what you need...

4 ounces/100 g butter • 4 ounces/100 g granulated sugar • Three medium organic eggs • Six drops of pure vanilla extract • One mixing bowl • Electric whisk • 8 ounces/225 g wholewheat/self-raising flour • 4 ounces/100 g mixed fruit and peel • 2 ounces/50 g glacé cherries • One level teaspoon of mixed spice • Three drops of rosewater • One 7 inch/ 18 cm-diameter cake tin • One yellow helium-filled balloon • One small cake skewer • Six pink cake candles and holders • Four pink candles, approximately 6 inches/15 cm in length, placed in secure holders • Matches or lighter

what to do...

◆ First, preheat the oven to 400°F/200°C. Then make the cake by placing the butter, sugar, eggs, and vanilla extract in the mixing bowl and beating with the electric whisk until pale. Add the flour and blend in the mixed fruit, cherries, mixed spice, and rosewater. Place the mixture in the cake tin and bake for approximately 15 minutes, or until golden brown and firm. Allow to cool.

◆ Place the cake and all the other ingredients on your dining table and visualize a circle of white light encompassing the whole room.

◆ Fasten the balloon tie to a skewer and anchor this to the middle of the cake, saying:
Always loved and always cherished
May this friendship never perish.

◆ Place the six cake candles in their holders on the cake.

◆ Place the four larger pink candles at an equal distance from each other around the cake, safely away from the balloon, saying:
Loving Venus, planet of harmony and affection
Bless my friendships
I wish for my friendship always to be
As precious to my
Friends as theirs is to me
As I will this, so mote it be!

◆ Light the four pink candles and wait for your friends to arrive, at which point, light the rest of the candles on the cake. Invite your friends to make a wish and blow these out collectively, and the wish will be carried into the ether to work its magic.

Honey sandwich spell

Staying friends with your neighbors

Our home is our sanctuary from the outside world, a place where we expect to be protected, nourished, and loved. However, the level to which this can be achieved may sometimes be determined as much by the people you live next door to as by those with whom you actually live. Good neighbors are undoubtedly a blessing; they will keep an eye on your home when you are away, feed the cat, water the plants, but never intrude. Bad neighbors, on the other hand, can make life hell.

This spell works on the notion of cementing good relationships with your neighbors. The two slices of bread represent the households of you and your neighbors respectively, while the honey symbolizes your desire to keep things sweet between you. Remember, though, that you also have to be a good neighbor. It's no good casting a spell to keep your neighbors friendly if you are annoying them by throwing noisy parties, playing loud music or forgetting to take in the garbage can! You could invite your neighbors in for a cup of coffee after you have cast this spell, and share some Friendship cake (see pages 46–47) with them!

Put this spell to the test on a waxing moon, to attract harmony and peace, and on a Friday, the day of the relationship planet, Venus.

what you need...

One green candle, approximately 6 inches/15 cm in length, placed in a secure holder • Matches or lighter • One small bunch of dried white sage leaves • One fireproof dish to hold the sage leaves • One tablespoon of clear honey • Two slices of wholewheat bread • One spoon • One knife

what to do...

- Place all the ingredients on your dining room table.
- Visualize a circle of hedges hemming the entire room, with an attractive gateway to the side that connects you with the neighbors about whom you are thinking.
- Keeping this vision in your mind's eye, light the candle, saying:
  Element of Earth,
  Strengthen the boundaries around this home
  And bless the spell that I intone.
- Light the edges of the sage leaves and blow them out, allowing them to smolder in the dish.
- Walk clockwise all around your dining room, censing the visualized hedges and gateway with the sweet smoke from the sage, and intoning the following words:
  Wisdom guide all

Whose boundaries meet mine,
My ways and their ways
Let wisdom combine.

- Return to the table and spread the honey on the two slices of bread, using the spoon, then sandwich the pieces together, and repeat the words used above to cense the circle of hedges.
- Cut the honey sandwich in half with the knife. Eat one half yourself, then go outside to your garden or yard, and crumble and sprinkle the other half all along the side of your property adjacent to your neighbor's house.
- Leave this for the birds to eat, then go back to your "circle" of hedges and spend a little time meditating on how you can be a good neighbor, before allowing the inner vision of your "hedgerow" to disperse.

Cooking and Healing

Kitchen spells

Forget the cauldron and the magic potion: the kitchen is where brews for

health and well-being are concocted these days. In this chapter you will find

a saucepanful of potions to nourish the body and soul, aid good health and

balance, help recovery after illness, assure abundance, and cleanse the home

of negative vibes. Happy brewing!

Bread spell

Nourishing the body and spirit

This spell is to aid your spiritual growth and well-being. It links physical and spiritual nourishment by using the art of bread-making. Don't worry if you have never made bread before: this spell offers a foolproof dried-yeast recipe, which produces delicious, wholesome bread every time!

There has always been something wonderful about the way that wheat growing in a field is transformed into one of the most familiar food-stuffs on our plates. Now that bread is more often bought from stores than baked at home, however, the link between field and table is not so obvious. Most of us are removed from the

experience of seeing that mysterious, living organism—yeast—help flour-and-water dough to double in size and rise in the oven.

Spiritual and personal development involves finding out about our place in the world and how that world operates. Making our own bread is, therefore, a good way of reconnecting with the mysterious processes that produce the grain, and then transform it into bread. You will also "enchant" the dough as you knead it, to give yourself some magical, as well as physical, nourishment.

Try this spell out during a waxing moon, preferably on a Monday, the day of the moon.

what you need...

One white candle, approximately 6 inches/15 cm in length, placed in a secure holder • Matches or a lighter
• 1½ pounds/750g wholemeal flour • One large mixing bowl • 1½ teaspoons (5 ml spoons) of salt
• 1 ounce/25 g shortening (white vegetable fat)
• ⅓ ounce/7 g dried yeast • ¾ pint/450 ml warm water
• One spoon • Spare flour for kneading • Clean cloth
• Large baking tray

what to do...

- Preheat the oven to 450°F/230°C.
- Place all the ingredients on the work surface in your kitchen.
- Light the candle, saying:
  I honor the Spirit of the grain
  Grown in earth by sun and rain
  May my body and spirit nourished be
  And grow in health and harmony.
- Place the flour in the bowl, mix in the salt, then rub in the shortening (fat) and add the yeast.
- Make a hole in the center of the mixture and pour in the warm water, stirring it with the spoon until the mixture is stiff.
- Flour the work surface and knead the dough firmly for about 15 minutes, chanting as you do so:
  Water my blood,
  Earth my flesh,
  Fire my spirit,
  Air my breath.
- Place the dough back into the bowl, cover with a clean cloth, and leave by the oven for approximately 50 minutes.
- Knead again for another 15 minutes, repeating the chant as before.
- Divide the dough into three, roll all three parts into long sausage shapes of equal length, then braid them together, and form them into a ring.
- Place the dough on a baking tray next to the oven for about 50 minutes, then bake in the center of the oven for 30–40 minutes until browned.
- Cut and eat a generous slice before the loaf is entirely cold, and crumble another slice outside for the birds.

Red handkerchief spell

Promoting good health

This spell uses common baking ingredients found in most super-markets and stores, so the items for this enchantment should be easy to assemble. Nutmeg, used here to symbolize health and heartiness, is also sometimes used in magic for protection. This makes it suitable for guarding, as well as promoting, health. Cloves and clove oil have a similar alternative use, as well as being used historically for toothaches. Here, cloves are used to symbolize protection from pain. Cinnamon, which is associated with the element of Fire, and with the Sun, was once used as a stimulant. In this spell it symbolizes vitality.

The color red is considered particularly lucky in some cultures. In China, gifts of cash are sometimes offered in a red envelope, giving rise to the saying that someone experiencing a rush of good fortune is having a "red-letter day." In the system of magic used in the West, red is associated with positive energy and the life force. Wrapping the magical ingredients in a red handkerchief for safekeeping is thus a good way of ensuring that you are fortunate in the areas of health and well-being.

Put this spell to the test on a Tuesday, the day of energetic Mars, and on a waxing moon, to attract and promote good health.

what you need...

One oil burner • Matches or a lighter • A little water • Three drops of cinnamon oil • One red candle, approximately 6 inches/15 cm in length, placed in a secure holder • One whole nutmeg • Five cloves • One cinnamon stick, cut into three equal lengths • One 6 inch/15 cm square of red satin • One 6 inch/15 cm length of ½ inch/1 cm-wide ribbon

what to do...

- Place all the ingredients on your kitchen table or work surface.
- Light the oil burner and warm the water and cinnamon oil.
- Light the candle, saying:
  I call upon the energy of Mars
  To guard, promote, and improve my health.
- Take the nutmeg and, passing it through the fumes of the heated oil, say:
  May I be whole and hearty.
- Next, take the cloves and do the same, this time saying:
  Free from pain and despair.
- Then repeat the action with the three pieces of cinnamon, saying:
  Instilled with the energy of the life force.
- Place all three ingredients in the center of the red satin "handkerchief," bringing the four corners of it together, and use the ribbon to fasten the objects within the handkerchief, leaving enough ribbon to form a loop.
- As you tie the ingredients firmly into the handkerchief, say clearly:
  So mote it be!
- Hang the pouch up in your kitchen from a high point, preferably near a window, where the sunlight can catch it and continue to energize your wishes.
- Repeat the spell using fresh ingredients whenever you wish to renew your health, energy, and general well-being.

Tea bag spell

Keeping health and harmony

Medical experts agree that the secret of good health is keeping a balance in all things, and living in peace with our surroundings. This spell is designed to help you do just that, using a conveniently modern way of producing a magical potion. The good news is that you don't need a witches' cauldron in which to brew this; a plain old teacup will do!

In most magical paths, the element of Water is associated with healing and emotional balance. In Celtic legend water from the Grail was reputed to heal the most mortal of wounds and diseases. In a contemporary twist on this tradition, we use the humble teacup to contain that most reviving and comforting of "brews"—tea. Mindful of health warnings related to excess caffeine and tannin, this spell recommends using fruit tea. Fruit teas are now available from most stores in tea bag form, and you should choose the flavor that most appeals to you. If you have not tried fruit tea before, stick to "red" or berry-type flavors, as these are most people's favorites. You may need to sweeten the tea to your taste with a little honey or sugar.

Try this spell on a waxing half-moon, on any day of the week, to ensure that a sense of balance is invoked.

what you need...

One teacup • One saucer • One teaspoon • One fruit tea bag • One black candle, approximately 6 inches/15 cm in length, placed in a secure holder • One white candle approximately 6 inches/15 cm in length, placed in a secure holder • Kettle of water • Matches or a lighter
• A little honey or sugar (optional)

what to do...

◆ Place the teacup on the saucer, with the spoon alongside them, on your kitchen table or work surface, together with the tea bag.

◆ Position the black candle to the left and the white candle to the right of the teacup.

◆ While you are waiting for the kettle to boil, visualize a circle of silver light encircling the entire kitchen.

◆ When the kettle boils, sit down and light the black candle, saying:
Powers of sleep and stillness,
Powers of rest and silence
Powers that are within me
I call you up.

◆ Light the white candle, saying:
Powers of awareness and creation
Powers of action and speech
Powers that are within me
I call you up.

◆ Close your eyes and visualize a half-moon in the sky, focusing on the perfect balance of light and darkness on the Moon's disk. Hold this image for the length of at least 30 heartbeats, then open your eyes.

◆ Pour the steaming water onto the tea bag in the teacup, and stir with the spoon. Sweeten as required.

◆ Imagine the balancing powers of the half-moon being poured into the brew as you stir, and chant the following words:
Heal my body, heal my soul,
Bring me balance, make me whole.

◆ Continue doing this until the tea is cool enough to drink, then drink it right down.

◆ Repeat this spell whenever you need to bring a sense of balance into the way you manage your life—and health.

Crystal spell

Recovering after illness

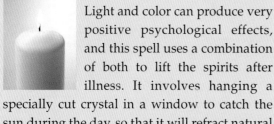

Light and color can produce very positive psychological effects, and this spell uses a combination of both to lift the spirits after illness. It involves hanging a specially cut crystal in a window to catch the sun during the day, so that it will refract natural sunlight and create rainbows inside the room. This would probably work best in a kitchen with a south-facing window. Alternatively, you can conduct the spell in the kitchen, then hang the crystal in a room that is more suitable for catching the sunlight, if you prefer.

Because of the pressures of modern life, we often neglect the recovery time that is needed

after serious illness. This can sometimes lead to feeling low and being susceptible to minor infections. This spell is designed to lift the spirits and induce further healing during convalescence. You could make a gift of the crystal to a friend or relative who is in recovery—or keep yourself cheered up by its colorful patterns.

Common sense and self-care are important factors in taking responsibility for your health. Although a little enchantment can aid your way to full recovery, you should seek medical advice and help if you are troubled by depression or recurring symptoms. Cast this spell on a waxing moon, on any day, with a Sunday providing the most favorable aspect for recovery.

what you need...

One cut crystal pendant, with a line attached • One dish of salt • One sewing needle • One white candle, approximately 6 inches/15 cm in length, placed in a secure holder • Matches or a lighter • One glass of natural spring water

what to do...

- Bury the crystal in salt for 24 hours prior to the casting of the spell, ensuring that the line is visible, ready for lifting the crystal out.
- Place all the ingredients on your kitchen table or work surface, with the crystal still buried in the salt.
- Visualize a circular rainbow entirely encompassing the kitchen.
- Take the needle and inscribe a diamond shape into one side of the candle.
- Inscribe your initial/the initial of the person you are helping into the other side of the candle.
- Light the candle, saying:
  May this aid [name]'s recovery:
  As I will it, so mote it be!
- Lift the crystal out of the salt by the line, without touching the crystal itself.
- Dip the crystal into the spring water, saying:
  Wash of water, purity of salt
  Stress and illness come to a halt.
- Concentrate on the crystal, visualizing yourself/your friend looking healthy and happy. Continue this for at least 60 heartbeats.
- Hang the crystal in the kitchen window, where it will create rainbows from the light of the sun and bring color healing into your life.

KITCHEN SPELLS

Soup spell

For your family's good health

This is a tasty spell, designed to bring good health to the entire family. As magic is an eminently practical craft, this involves cooking up a delicious meal with ingredients that are health-giving as well as magically symbolic. As usual, the recipe involves items that have slightly more arcane meanings than are realized in their everyday use, and these are explained in each of the rhymes with which you pop them into the pot!

This spell works best if you can get everyone to sit down to eat together at the same time—no mean feat in a busy family situation. Needless to say, the ingredients have also been chosen for their nutritional content. Good nutrition has never been a great enticement to youngsters, so it might be fun to get the children to help you with this spell, especially if they are fussy about eating vegetables. Helping out in the kitchen, and watching an adult speak rhymes over the ingredients, might encourage them to taste some of them out of sheer curiosity. Not many kids get to eat a magic carrot, after all! This quantity serves four, so adjust it according to your own requirements.

Throw this spell into the pot on a waxing moon to attract good health, on any day, with Sunday ("Sun's Day") being the favorite.

what you need...

One large pot • 3 teaspoons/15 ml of vegetable oil • One wooden spoon • ½ English onion, finely chopped • 4 cloves garlic, chopped • 1½ pounds/750 g potatoes, peeled and chopped • 1½ pounds/750 g tomatoes, chopped • 1½ pounds/750 g carrots, scrubbed and chopped • 1½ pints/900 ml hot water/vegetable stock • Blender • Salt and pepper to taste • Two red candles, any length, placed in secure holders • Matches or a lighter

what to do...

- ◆ Place the pot over a medium heat, then heat the oil and, using the wooden spoon, stir in the ingredients in the order stipulated below, ensuring that each glazes slightly before the next ingredient is added.
- ◆ Add onions, saying:
  For contentment, not tears.
- ◆ Throw in the garlic, saying:
  For protection, not fear.
- ◆ Add the potatoes, saying:
  Be strong, not weak.
- ◆ Add the tomatoes, saying:
  Be fearless, not meek.
- ◆ Put in the carrots, saying:
  Shine brightly, not dim.
- ◆ Then pour in the water/stock, saying:
  Stir these round and blend them in.
- ◆ When these ingredients are cooked, wait for them to cool down a little, then mix them to a smooth purée in the blender before returning the pan to the heat.
- ◆ Flavor the soup with salt and pepper, saying:
  Strength and sweetness balanced thus
  Within this soup and within us!
- ◆ Place the two candles on the table, and light them, saying:
  May vitality and energy be gained by what is eaten at this meal.
- ◆ Serve up the soup when it is hot, accompanied by chunks of bread—perhaps made to the recipe for the Bread spell (see pages 52–53).

Floral candle spell

Ensuring abundance in your life

Most people in ordinary households have to ensure that they have enough money to pay their rent or mortgage, pay their bills, and put food on the table. Worrying about cash for the basics can lead to anxiety, stress, and—if it is prolonged—ill health. This spell aims to keep the flow of material abundance pouring into your home, ensuring freedom from this type of worry as far as possible. It is not a cure-all for either hard times or frivolous housekeeping, so common sense needs to go hand in hand with spell casting.

Material abundance is ruled by the element of Earth, so a green candle and various plants are used here to symbolize the growth and fertility associated with Earth energy. If you are an avid gardener, you may find all the requisite items in your own garden or windowbox. Otherwise, most of them are available in the wild, or from a florist or garden center. The greenery arrangement should last for at least seven days, and possibly longer, provided that you remember to add a little cold water to the foam base each day.

Bring abundance into your home, and your life, by casting your magic on a waxing or Full Moon, preferably on a Monday, the day traditionally associated with money.

what you need...

One small block of wet (green) florist's foam
• One saucer • Several strands of ivy, any variety
• Several sprigs of evergreens, any variety • One bunch of mint • Six flowers, any that are in season • One green candle, approximately 8 inches/20 cm in length
• Half a tumbler of cold water

what to do...

- Place all ingredients on your kitchen table or work surface.
- Cut the florist's foam to fit onto the saucer, then position it there.
- Visualize a plant emerging from the floor of your kitchen, and growing until its stalk reaches the ceiling, and its leaves cascade outward and curve down the walls to touch the floor.
- Keeping this image in your mind's eye, poke the root end of the ivy strands into the foam. When you have tucked the last one in, say:
  Ivy for tenacity, and growth in barren times.
- Do the same with the other evergreens, working your way around the foam to form a balanced arrangement, saying:
  Evergreens for endurance, and neverending flow.

- Now tuck the mint into the foam, stalk first, saying:
  Mint for riches, old and new.
- Finish off the arrangement by spacing the flowers equally around the foam, saying:
  May all that is good in life flourish and grow.
- Push the base of the candle firmly into the center of the foam so that it is securely anchored, then light it, saying:
  Spirits of Earth, rock and root, stalk and leaf
  Provide all I/we need beneath this roof.
- Wet the foam with the water, and add a little water every day for seven days.
- Ensure that the candle is lit in the kitchen at sundown for an hour on seven consecutive nights, replacing it with a new green candle whenever it burns down to greenery level.

Garlic spell

Cleansing your home of negative energies

Sometimes busy homes can collect the stresses and anxious feelings of everyday cares (including those introduced by visitors to the house) and can occasionally create an atmosphere that is less than happy and healthy. This means that it is time for a good, old-fashioned psychic clean sweep; enter the humble clove of garlic.

You might be surprised to know that the vampire lore created in 1960s horror movies actually got something right in relation to magical symbolism: garlic, used in the movies to ward off vampires, is traditionally employed to purify and fend off bad vibes. As most

herbalists know, concentrated quantities of garlic act as a natural antibiotic. What most magicians know is that garlic is a great cleanser on the psychic level, too.

This spell requires you to smear all the glass surfaces in your home with some raw garlic: including mirrors, glazed photographs, pictures, and windows. You should include any surface by which light comes into your home, or is reflected. The idea is that garlic purifies all energy that enters your home, which in a short time neutralizes and overcomes the bad atmosphere that has accumulated. Try to cast this spell on a waning or New Moon. Saturday, the day of Saturn the banisher, is best.

what you need...

Four cloves of garlic, peeled and cut in half horizontally
• One saucer • One black candle, approximately
6 inches/15 cm in length, placed in a secure holder
• Matches or a lighter • One bowl containing
approximately 6 fluid ounces/175 ml of spring water
• One bowl containing approximately 1 dessertspoon
of salt

what to do...

◆ Place all the ingredients on your kitchen table or work surface, with the freshly peeled and cut garlic cloves on the saucer.

◆ Light the candle, saying:
I banish worry, envy, anger from this place.

◆ Take the water and sprinkle it over the garlic, saying:
May you cleanse all that enters here.

◆ Take the salt and sprinkle it over the garlic, saying:
May the good that enters in
Drive out all the bad it finds.

◆ Then take the dish of garlic cloves to every room in the house, rubbing the cut end of the cloves over every glass surface that you find.

◆ When this is accomplished, return to the kitchen.

◆ Focusing your attention on the candle, imagine the light from the flame reaching out to all areas of your home, growing in brilliance until it chases away all shadows. Visualize the bad atmosphere as dark smoke, evaporating and leaving through the windows, mirrors, and glass surfaces of your home. Then see sunlight flowing back in through those same surfaces, cleansing and brightening your home.

◆ Place the garlic on a saucer outside your home. When the cloves have dried up completely, bury them in soil away from the building.

I am here in Peace
I am Safe and Secure
I create with Love
I Accept myself
My heart is Open
I speak my Truth
I trust my Intuition
I am Divine Being
I am here in Peace

Creating

l s

The study is where we do much of our thinking, problem solving, and sorting out of organizational chores. It is mental, as well as physical, space that concerns us in this chapter. Over the next pages you will discover spells for enhancing your mental, creative, and intuitive powers, for getting organized, increasing your concentration, and finding success in applications, tests, and interviews.

STUDY SPELLS

Bead spell

Promoting mental agility

There are times when we all feel a little jaded or unimaginative, and in need of a mental boost. Try this spell when your brain stalls and refuses to spark—it really does work wonders.

The use of beads to help focus the attention on a task is well established. Worry beads, popular in the 1970s, came from a tradition where your worries could be transferred into the beads, and handling them when stressed was a way of relaxing. Rosary and sutra beads are used in religious traditions to help adherents focus on their prayers and chants. In this spell, beads are used to initiate a free flow of ideas and thoughts.

It is important that you make your own beads, because the creative energies that form them are a significant aspect of encouraging your personal creative thought processes. You can make them from a plastic modeling clay or from self-hardening clay, which can be found in most craft stores. If you use a plastic clay that needs to be hardened in an oven, be careful to use the appropriate colors and follow the instructions on the package for baking times. Self-hardening clay beads will need to be handpainted and varnished when they have set.

Cast this spell on a waxing moon to attract mental agility, and on a Wednesday, the day of Mercury the communicator.

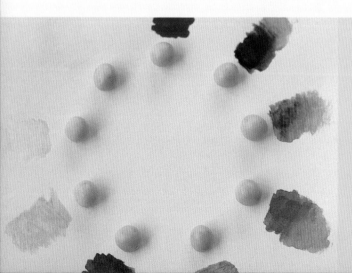

what you need...

Sufficient plastic modeling clay in the colors given below, or self-hardening clay, to make nine beads • Paint (if using self-hardening clay) in the following colors: black, blue, green, purple, red, yellow, white, silver, and gold • Varnish (if using self-hardening clay) • Newspaper to work on • One yellow candle, approximately 6 inches/15 cm in length, placed in a secure holder • Matches or a lighter • 15 inch/38 cm length of fine black cord

what to do...

◆ Prior to casting the spell, you need to fashion nine beads of equal size from your chosen material: one of each color, with a hole through them large enough to accommodate the cord you will be using. Paint and varnish them as necessary, working on the newspaper. Assemble all the materials in your study when the beads are ready.

◆ Light the candle, saying:
I invoke the powers of Mercury,
The powers of swift thought
And clear expression
To aid my spell.

◆ Tie a knot in one end of the cord and thread the beads on in the following order, invoking the property of each as you do so:
Black for creativity
Blue for ease of flow
Green for natural growth
Purple for expanding knowledge
Red for inspiration
Yellow for expression
White for focus
Silver for intuition
Gold for reason.

◆ Fasten a knot at the other end of the cord and, holding the beads up before the candle, say:
Three for my thoughts and
Three times three
To magnify ability.

◆ Keep the beads close to you in your study, and handle them to help you concentrate whenever you need a magical mental "boost."

STUDY SPELLS

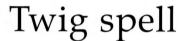

Twig spell

Success in examinations, tests, and interviews

Even the best-prepared candidates need a little luck to give them the edge when it comes to exams, tests, and interviews. Carrying a talisman that is magically charged to aid your abilities in such situations is psychologically comforting, as well as magically empowering.

For this spell you need a naturally forked twig. Go outside to find a twig that has fallen from a tree—you should not cut one from a living plant for this spell—and fashion it to fit you and your intentions. The twig will be carried in your pocket or handbag, so you may need to cut it down to size. Naturally forked branch formations have traditionally been used as staffs placed in the ground to mark territory, and for hanging or marking lucky symbols and signs on. In this spell you will be marking a job or a qualification as your rightful property, and carrying a little luck with you.

Needless to say, this spell will not help you succeed if you have not worked to deserve the job, qualification, or accolade that you seek. But it will help give you the edge in getting the exam mark, test result, college place, or job that is right for you. Try your luck by casting this spell on a waxing moon to draw you toward your goal, on a Wednesday for communication energy or a Thursday for good fortune.

what you need...

One oil burner • A little water • Three drops of benzoin essential oil • Three drops of cinnamon essential oil • One yellow candle, approximately 6 inches/15 cm in length, placed in a secure holder • Matches or a lighter • One purple candle, approximately 6 inches/15 cm in length, placed in a secure holder • One sharp craft or kitchen knife • One naturally forked twig • One 6 inch/15 cm length of plain string or twine

what to do...

- Place all the ingredients on the desk in your study on a surface where you have been researching or studying for your exam/test/interview.
- Light the oil burner, placing the water and essential oils in its dish.
- Light the yellow candle, saying:
  Mercury ease my
  Way in this exam/test/interview.
- Light the purple candle, saying:
  Jupiter bring me
  Fortune.
- Using the craft knife, trim the forked twig to a convenient size to fit in your pocket or handbag.
- Then carve into the longest part of the twig the rune known as "Rad." (See illustration, page 124.) Rad means "wheel," and it will help the wheel of fortune turn in your favor.
- Now slowly wind the string or twine around the base of the twig, chanting as you do so:
  Air to find,
  Thread to bind,
  Find what's best and
  Make it mine.
- Tie off the string and the spell is complete.
- Carry the twig with you when you attend your exam/test/interview, and keep it close to you until you have achieved your goal. Afterward, say a silent "Thank you" as you cast it into flowing water.

Acorn spell

Finding inspiration

When you are stuck with a problem to solve, or are required to be imaginative or creative, it can be frustrating waiting for a flash of inspiration to come to you. This is particularly true when the things that usually spark your imagination draw a blank. This spell will help you to find that elusive source of creativity by making a magical talisman from which to draw inspiration when you are stuck.

The talisman in question is an acorn. Not only does it symbolize the potential of huge growth from a tiny seed, but it comes from a tree traditionally associated with lightning: the oak. The ancient gods and goddesses of lightning, and other sources of fire power, such as the Sun, were often associated with the oak. In the Celtic tree alphabet, and in old Norse traditions, the oak is seen as having solar characteristics, and is linked with the Sun, Fire, and storm deities. This makes the acorn the perfect symbol of fortuitous creativity, as it represents the lightning strike of sudden inspiration and is itself a small source of great things.

Test this spell on a waxing moon, and on a Tuesday, the day of the god or goddess known as Tiuw, or on a Thursday in honor of the thunder god Thor.

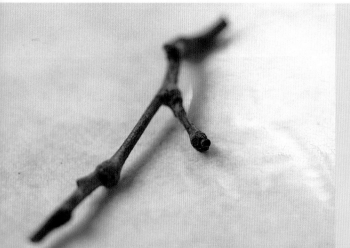

what you need...

One sharp-pointed iron nail, any length • One red candle, approximately 6 inches/15 cm in length, placed in a secure holder • Matches or a lighter • One intact acorn, complete with cup • Half a glass of milk (dairy or soya) • One twig 5–9 inches/13–23 cm in length, dropped from an oak tree

what to do...

- Place all the ingredients on the desk in your study, or on the surface that you generally use for the work for which you are seeking inspiration.
- Visualize a ring of white light entirely encompassing the study.
- Take the nail and, using the point, carve into the side of the candle a zigzag shape to represent a fork of lightning, and the shape of an upward-pointing arrow, symbol of the oak tree.
- Light the candle, saying:
  Spirit of flame
  Might of the oak
  Combine to bring forth
  The sudden light of inspiration.
- Take the acorn and anoint it with a little milk from the glass, then drink the rest of the milk.
- Take the oak twig in your writing hand, and the acorn in the other, and point the twig directly at the acorn, saying:
  I charge this seed,
  Empowered with nourishment,
  To contain the inspiration
  That strikes suddenly,
  To contain the fire
  That burns brightly,
  To contain the spark
  That sets the imagination alight.
- Now enclose the acorn in both hands, and visualize yourself busy at your writing/craft/work, using bright ideas and expressing them freely.
- Keep the acorn in the place where you usually carry out the work for which you require inspiration, and cup it in both hands whenever you need this. Stay very still and quiet, and wait for inspiration to come.

Seashell spell

Enhancing intuition

In your studies, or any kind of endeavor requiring concentration, intuition is often as important as the use of reason and logic. Intuition has been vastly under-valued in recent centuries; this remarkable ability has often been written off as "luck" or "guessing." Sometimes seen as the domain of women, and therefore dismissed as a "feminine" trait in male-dominated societies, intuition in fact represents a good nine-tenths of creativity, and thus of pro-ductivity. If you wish to maximize your intuitive powers, then this is the spell for you.

In magic, the power of intuition is associated with the tides of the Moon and the sea. The waters of the Earth, tied to our nearest celestial neighbor by the power of gravity, react to the movement of that body around our planet. Although the pull of the Moon's gravity is invisible to us, we perceive that water reacts to its very real force. This is perhaps similar to the concept we have of intuition: although it is not apparent and obvious, there is a deep knowledge by which we know how things are going to turn out if we take certain actions. This enchantment uses shells, archetypal symbols of the sea, to represent intuition.

Work on a Monday, the day of the Moon, and when it is waxing, to bring about the full flow of your intuitive powers.

what you need...

One blue candle, approximately 7–8 inches/18–20 cm in length, placed in a secure holder • Matches or a lighter • One sharp needle or a fine craft drill bit • Three scallop-type seashells • One blue felt-tipped pen • Blue cotton thread • Hammer • One masonry nail

what to do...

- Place all the ingredients on the desk in your study, or on your general work surface in whichever room you usually carry out the hobby, work, or study for which you most need to develop your intuitive powers.
- Visualize the whole room surrounded by water.
- Light the blue candle, saying:

  Cycle of the Moon
  Tides of the sea
  May deep intuition
  Flow swiftly in me.

- Using the needle point or drill bit, carefully drill a small hole at the top of each of the shells. The "top" is the point at which the shell was once joined to its other half.
- Take the felt-tipped pen and draw two horizontal and parallel wavy lines on the inside of the first shell.

- On the second shell, draw a waxing crescent moon (the convex curve should face the same way as the bracket at the end of this line).
- On the third shell, draw a downward-pointing equilateral triangle.
- Thread the cotton through all three shells, then tie it in a loop.
- Cup the shells in your hands and concentrate, for 60 heartbeats, on the image of the water you have visualized surrounding the room.
- Hammer the nail into a wall or post in the room close to where you usually do your concentrating, and hang up the shells.
- Whenever your intuitive powers need a boost, concentrate on the shells for a few minutes, visualizing water completely surrounding you.

Sand bowl spell

Promoting organization in your life

Normally, when you cast a spell, you should leave the ingredients undisturbed in order for the spell to "take." This spell is specifically designed to enable you to reactivate and change it from day to day.

The most effective organization depends on a certain flexibility of thought. Whereas some tasks need a stiff, formal framework of organization, others require a more subtle approach. With this spell you will be able to choose which approach is most suited to the tasks you have in hand. This is why the archetypal symbol of shifting bases—sand—is used as the key material.

Once the spell is initiated, you will be able to change the shapes you trace in the sand to meet the needs of the moment. If you need to be highly organized and disciplined, you can draw a square to represent logical thought. If you need to be more creative, you can draw a spiral to represent lateral thought. Waves and curves tend to signify intuitive, creative thinking, whereas squares and straight lines symbolize more ordered, sequential thought. It would be a good idea to meditate on concepts associated with different shapes in the preparation for this spell. Cast this spell on a waxing moon, preferably on a Wednesday, which is associated with Mercury and the Air element, to emphasize thinking.

what you need...

One yellow candle, approximately 6 inches/15 cm in length, placed in a secure holder • Matches or a lighter • A large shallow bowl, at least 8 inches/20 cm in diameter (the type used for floating candles would be ideal) • Sufficient decorative or silver sharp (sandpit) sand to almost fill the bowl • One large bird feather, shed naturally

what to do...

- ◆ Assemble all the ingredients on your study desk or worktop.
- ◆ Light the candle and, focusing on the flame, visualize its light spreading throughout and beyond the room, until it forms a huge light globe encompassing the whole area.
- ◆ Pour the sand into the bowl, and shake it gently to achieve a smooth surface.
- ◆ Press the palm of your writing hand down on the surface of the sand, saying:
  My imprint upon this sand
  Made by mine, and no other's hand.
- ◆ Shake the bowl gently to regain a smooth surface once more.

- ◆ Take the feather, and use its tip to inscribe into the sand the shape that represents the type of organizational approach (see left) that you will need at the next sunrise.
- ◆ Leave this undisturbed until the following sunset, after which you are free to inscribe at any time the shape of the thought patterns required by you.
- ◆ It is recommended that you expand your repertoire of symbols and shapes associated with your organizational approaches and thought processes by frequent meditation over the next moon cycle. Over time you can incorporate more personal and subtle shifts of approach, as required.

STUDY SPELLS

Pine tree spell

Increasing concentration

Even the most diligent of us can fail assignments, miss deadlines, or feel blocked when our powers of concentration elude us. When the reason for such lack of concentration is known, it is generally simple to remedy. Tiredness or illness can be remedied by sleep and cures, and distraction by noise can be resolved by moving to a quieter location. However, when the cause is less apparent, a little magical effort may be required.

Some people wonder whether magic is more "psychology" than anything else and they are about 90 percent right. The mind is a very powerful tool. Witches and magicians often define magic as "that which connects," and since our mental faculties make important connections between ourselves and the world, the workings of the mind can be defined as magical, too. Just because a spell can have a profoundly positive psychological effect doesn't make it any less magical! This spell appeals to our psychological and physiological selves to be still and to focus for a while. The scents of pine and lavender, both of which are used in this spell, are known to have a positive effect on our ability to concentrate.

Test this spell on a waxing moon to increase your concentration, and on a Wednesday, the day of Mercury the communicator.

what you need...

One lavender-scented candle, any size or shape, or one tea light (or votive) with a couple of drops of lavender essential oil added • Matches or a lighter • Three fresh pine sprays, with leaves intact • One 6 inch/15 cm length of narrow yellow ribbon • Three drops of pine essential oil

what to do...

- Gather all the ingredients in your study or in the main "brainwork" space in your home.

- Light the candle or tea light (or votive), saying:
  Power of scent
  Of relaxation
  Aid my powers of
  Concentration.

- Allow the candle to burn for a while and to scent the space in which you are working, breathing in the aroma deeply.

- Take the pine sprays and fasten them toward the cut ends with the yellow ribbon, leaving a loop by which to hang the bunch when the spell is completed.

- Drip the pine essential oil onto the ribbon by which the sprays are fastened together, saying:
  Element of Air
  I summon and call you
  To enlarge my ability to be
  Still and focus
  To expand my ability to absorb and process knowledge
  Let it be so
  By my will.

- Hold the pine sprays in both hands, and fix your vision on the point at which it is fastened. Banish everything from your mind that does not directly relate to the knotted ribbon around the sprays, and remain so for at least 60 heartbeats.

- Hang the pine sprays in your study, or keep them near you during any task for which you need to concentrate—and stay focused!

Mail spell

To attain a successful outcome to a request, application, or complaint

Achieving a positive outcome to an application, a request, or a letter of complaint is simple with this spell, which is designed to enhance your chances of success. The purpose of your original missive—be it by post, e-mail, or via the Internet—can be almost anything, as long as it is not unreasonable, rude, or unethical, for this spell is flexible enough to accommodate all types of concern.

Before casting this spell, you should ensure that your request, application, or complaint and its desired outcome are clear, both in the communication that you are intending to send out and in your own mind. If you are not a great letter writer, get a friend to check it over to ensure that your message is clear and persuasive. Be certain that you are in the right, especially if you are asking for magical help with a complaint or a request for justice! If it is a job or college application, ensure that this really is what you want and that you are suited and properly qualified, before setting pen to paper or finger to keyboard. Otherwise, no amount of magic will get you what you want, or make you happy with the outcome.

Cast your magic on a waxing moon to bring forward positive results, on any day of the week, with Wednesday being best for communication success.

what you need...

One silver candle, any length, placed in a secure holder • Matches or a lighter • One large bird feather, shed naturally • One small disk of silver foil approximately 3 inches/7.5 cm in diameter • Fountain pen with any colored ink • One envelope • Writing paper • One postage stamp

what to do...

- Place all the ingredients on your writing desk or table.
- Light the silver candle, saying:
  Mercury, quicksilver
  Supple and fast-flowing
  Carry my message
  Coming and going.
- Visualize a silver sphere encompassing the room in which you are casting the spell.
- Take the feather and, using its tip, press into the foil disk the shape of a circle with a cross joined to the bottom, and an upward-pointing crescent joined to the top. This is the sign of the planet Mercury—also the name of a metal otherwise known as "quicksilver."
- Then, using the fountain pen, address the envelope to yourself, either at home or at work—whichever is most appropriate to the request you are sending.
- Next, write on the notepaper the following words:
  Dear [your name],
  I am writing to inform you that your request for [result you wish to achieve] has been granted and will be dealt with immediately, in a way that gives the most positive outcome for you.
  Yours truly,
  The Powers That Be
- Put this note into the envelope, attach the stamp, and mail the letter as soon as possible.
- When you receive it, put it in a safe place until the result you desire has been successfully attained, then burn it.

Loving and Dreaming

Bedroom spells

Our bedrooms are the place where we are perhaps most truly

ourselves. In this chapter you will find spells for healthy sleep and happy

dreams, as well as spells to protect a relationship, help you find love, and to

promote passion and fertility. All the spells are designed to enhance and

bless the place in which you do your loving and dreaming.

Dream Catcher spell

Creating a space for happy dreaming

The idea of the Dream Catcher as a magical net that captures bad dreams derives from Native American spirituality. Here, it is used as a symbol of the magic that is woven in this spell for happy dreams. The Dream Catcher acts as a sieve that sorts out the good dreams from the bad. It captures the latter in its net and holds them there until the first light of day dissolves their power. As anyone who has ever suffered from nightmares will know, the morning light is very effective for sweeping aside the fears of the night!

Although this spell is primarily done to create a space for happy dreams, it can also be used proactively to counter nightmares in adults. Before casting it, however, consider the reasons why they may be occurring. If you are on medication, check with your medical advisor. If the dreams are persistent and distressing and you cannot pinpoint their source, talk them over with a counselor. However, if you are experiencing upheaval in your life, the dreams may be providing you with guidance about the way you are responding to change, and you should listen to what they are telling you.

This spell can be cast on a waxing or Full Moon, as you are attracting dreams into the magical net you are weaving. Monday, the day of the Moon, is ideal.

what you need...

One white or silver candle, approximately 6 inches/15 cm in length, in a secure holder • Matches or a lighter • One willow hoop, approximately 12 inches/30 cm in diameter (available from craft stores and florists) • 4 feet/1.5 m of wool • 8 feet/2.5 m narrow turquoise satin ribbon • 8 feet/2.5 m narrow white satin ribbon • Scissors or a sharp knife • Three white or gray bird feathers, shed naturally • Six large white beads, bought or made • Three leaves of dried white sage • One fireproof dish

what to do...

- Gather all the ingredients into the center of the room in which you will be working.
- Light the candle, saying:
  Sister Moon, bright while we are sleeping
  I entrust [my/friend's name] dreams into your
  good keeping.
- Visualize a ring of white light encircling the room.
- Secure the end of the wool to the willow hoop.
- Stretch it across the center of the hoop, then secure it to the hoop as necessary to make a pattern in the center that forms a web or net of any shape.
- As you are weaving, empower your Dream Catcher by chanting:
  Web of dreams
  Woven true
  Capture bad
  Let good pass through.

- When your center "web" or "net" is completed, fasten the wool off.
- Wind the turquoise ribbon around the hoop at regular intervals of approximately 2½ inches/6 cm, then fasten it off. Repeat with the white ribbon, making an alternating pattern, as shown in the illustration above.
- With the scissors or knife, cut the remaining ribbon into five equal lengths, double them over, and tie them together around the hoop.
- Tie the feathers and thread the beads onto these lengths, as shown.
- Light the dried sage in the fireproof dish, blow out the flames, and allow it to smolder.
- Cense your Dream Catcher with the smoke from the sweet sage, and then hang it in the window of your bedroom.

BEDROOM SPELLS

Dream pillow spell

Aiding restful sleep

The stresses of modern life often lead to situations that need a little old-fashioned help in the shape of herbs. As anybody with any herbal knowledge will tell you, lavender is one of the great "universal" remedies. One of its many uses is to aid relaxation and sleep, and this spell has the added benefit of creating an herb sachet that has practical as well as magical properties. Sleep should come easily, and so should pleasant dreams. As this is a natural remedy, it has none of the morning drowsiness associated with sleeping pills.

If you do not grow and harvest your own lavender, you should be able to obtain a sachet from outlets that sell herbs, potpourri, or dried flowers. You will need only a couple of handfuls for the Dream Pillow, so it should not be expensive, either. This spell produces something that you can offer someone else as a gift; naturally, a little expertise in sewing or embroidery can add to the appearance of the Dream Pillow, if you wish to prepare it well in advance of casting the spell. Embroidering a sprig of lavender or a waxing moon crescent on it, in lavender-colored thread, would be a particularly apt touch!

This spell should be cast on a waxing moon, to attract rest and health. Monday, day of the dream-weaving Moon, is best.

what you need...

One blue or white candle, approximately 6 inches/15 cm in length, placed in a secure holder • Matches or a lighter • Two handfuls of dried lavender in a bowl • Two oblong pieces of natural linen, approximately 6 x 4 inches/15 x 10 cm, stitched together firmly on three sides and turned outside in • One teaspoon • One fine embroidery needle • 12 inches/30 cm white sewing thread • 30 inches/75 cm double-threaded length of lavender embroidery silk • Scissors

what to do...

- Place all the ingredients in the center of the space in which you will be working.
- Light the candle, envisioning the light from it creating a protective sphere all around the room.
- Placing both hands palm down on the lavender in the bowl, visualize healing and restful energy flowing through your arms from your heart into the lavender. As you do this, chant or sing (finding your own tune):
  Mother Moon,
  Queen of dreaming,
  Bring [me/her/him] rest,
  While [I am/s/he is] sleeping.

- When you have chanted this at least nine times, spoon the lavender into the linen sachet and sew up the remaining open seam using the white thread.
- Recommencing your chant, and using the lavender thread, overstitch the seams of the sachet at approximately ½ inch/1 cm intervals all around it. Fasten off the thread.
- Hold the sachet in front of the candlelight, saying:
  As my thread around this spell is bound,
  So may sleep and rest gather around.
- The Dream Pillow can be held and sniffed, or kept on or under a pillow at night, according to preference. Sweet dreams!

Mustard spell

Promoting passion in your partner

Heard the expression "sharp as mustard?" Well, that's the point of this spell, which is designed to inspire passion in your partner. If your love life needs a boost, cast this spell and enjoy the results.

The use of mustard to heat the passions has a long history. The doctrine of signatures, which linked a plant's appearance with its medicinal effects, favored the bright yellow of mustard as a plant of light and heat. Village wise-women of the seventeenth century, noting the hot, burning sensation produced by its taste, prescribed mustard baths and poultices as remedies for colds and chills. In sympathetic magic, which is the representation of "like with like," mustard is used to symbolize heat. Applied to the notion of romance and physical desire, it is the natural ingredient to ignite passion, which is traditionally seen as "hot." Today, we still use heat to describe lust: we apply the term "red-hot," and refer to the "heat of desire." In this spell, mustard is used both as a magical symbol and as a natural aphrodisiac, for you will feed the results to your lover! If you don't have a pestle and mortar, use a bowl and spoon.

To help things go with a zing, this spell is best cast on a waxing moon, to maximize attraction, and either on Tuesday, the day of fiery Mars, or Friday, the day of passionate Venus.

what you need...

One red candle, approximately 6 inches/15 cm in length, placed in a secure holder • Matches or a lighter • One heaped teaspoon of dry mustard powder • One pestle and mortar • Couple of drops of spring water • One teaspoon • One pepper grinder containing whole black peppercorns • Plastic wrap (clingfilm)

what to do...

- Prepare this spell no more than 24 hours before you have the opportunity to feed the results to your partner.
- Gather all your ingredients in the center of your bedroom.
- Visualize a ring of flame encircling the room.
- Light the candle, saying:
  Element of Fire,
  Spirit of desire
  Witness my desire
  To stoke love's fire!
- Place the teaspoonful of dried mustard in the mortar, and grind and stir it with the pestle, visualizing all the while your partner approaching you with passionate intent. While you are grinding the powder, chant the following:
  Mustard hot
  Blended be
  Make my lover
  Ache for me.
- When you have chanted this rhyme several times, you will notice energy building within you. Direct this force through the pestle into the mustard you are stirring.
- When your instincts tell you that the mustard is "loaded" with the fiery energy you are sending into it, add a drop or two of spring water to the powder and stir it with the teaspoon to make a fine, smooth, paste.
- Grind a little black pepper onto the paste for extra heat, then cover it with plastic wrap (clingfilm) until you are able to spread it on a sandwich or add it to a meal that you are preparing for your lover.
- Now that you have lit the fuse, enjoy the fireworks!

Harmony wreath spell

Promoting harmony in your relationship

This is a happy spell, intended to bless a relationship with the harmony that so often makes love matches successful. It uses red and pink roses, renowned respectively as signs of passionate love and affection. In addition, it employs the symbolism of evergreens to bless the relationship with continual vitality. The circle shape of the wreath signifies the eternal nature of true love, while the material from which it is made—the willow—is strongly associated with Water, the element of love and balance.

If you are reading this spell because your relationship is going through a rough patch, you may need to do a bit more work before the spell is cast. Certainly a little magic can help, but it cannot hold together an ailing relationship. You will need to provide favorable circumstances for the spell to have a chance of success, by being very honest with yourself and your partner, and trying to work out why your partnership is in trouble. If you can work toward resolving difficult issues together and can arrive at workable solutions, this spell can be cast as a way of marking your joint future intentions to create harmony.

It should be cast on a waxing moon to draw harmony toward you, and on a Friday, the day of the peace-and-love planet Venus.

what you need...

Six red roses, slightly opened • Six pink roses, slightly opened • Pruning shears • 12 feet/3.6 m fine green wire • Green florist's tape • Fronds of yew, ivy, or other evergreen plants • One red candle, approximately 6 inches/15 cm in length, placed in a secure holder • Matches or a lighter • One willow hoop (available from craft stores and florists), about 8 inches/20 cm in diameter across the center • 7¼ feet/2.3 m of 1½ inch/4 cm-wide red satin ribbon

what to do...

- Trim the rose stalks with the shears to 2 inches/5 cm from the base of the flower heads. Wind pieces of fine wire around the bases and stalks, leaving 4 inches/10 cm of wire trailing from the stalk ends. Attach pieces of florists' tape and wire to the evergreen fronds.
- Gather all the ingredients in the center of your bedroom.
- Light the candle, saying:
  Venus, bright star of peace and harmony
  Shine favors down upon my love and me
  That we may grow in love and unity.
- Attach evergreens all the way around the front of the willow hoop, then fix roses evenly to it in an alternating pattern of red and pink.
- Attach the red ribbon to the hoop and wind it at 2½ inch/6 cm intervals all around, taking care not to flatten out the greenery too much or cover the roses.
- As you wind the ribbon, visualize the couple in question looking happy together, and send the warm feeling that this vision gives you from your heart into your hands, then through your fingers into the ribbon.
- Tie the remaining ribbon in a decorative bow at the base of the hoop.
- Hold the hoop aloft and declare:
  May [we/they] be shelter for each other,
  And never overshadow the other,
  And may [we/they] one and one be two together.
- Hang the Harmony Wreath above the bed.

Corn goddess spell

Aiding fertility

This spell is intended for those who are having trouble conceiving, when there is no medical reason why this should happen. It is based on the ancient tradition of catching the spirit of fertile growth and keeping it in the home until the crops come again. In this spell, the same principle is applied to human fertility—and here the spirit called upon is none other than the Earth goddess Demeter.

From the time when cereal crops were first cultivated, humans revered a goddess of fertility. The ancient Greeks worshipped Demeter (also known by the Romans as Ceres). Hellenic legends held that Demeter's grief for her missing daughter, Persephone, caused her to neglect the Earth's plant life and so created the first winter. When Persephone emerged from the Underworld, where she had been in the land of the dead, Demeter's rejoicing caused the Earth to burst into greenery and the crops to flourish again.

Demeter's role as tender of the greenery on Earth make her a natural deity of all kinds of fertility. Keeping a corn doll representing Demeter will hopefully attract her energies and favor your chances of conceiving. Cast this spell on a waxing moon for growth, and on a Monday, the day of the Moon, which governs women's cycles and reproduction.

what you need...

Four white tea lights (or votives) in holders • A little water • Six drops of patchouli essential oil • One oil burner with a tea light • Matches or a lighter • One green candle, approximately 6 inches/15 cm in length, placed in a secure holder • One bunch of corn, approximately one hand span in circumference • 9 feet/2.7 m of twine • 6 feet/1.8m of ½ inch/1 cm-wide dark green ribbon

what to do...

◆ Place the four tea lights (or votives) in holders at the East, South, West, and North points of the compass around the space in which you will be working, either on the floor or on tables, shelves, or windowsills (whichever is safest).

◆ Move the remainder of the ingredients to the center of the room. Place the water and essential oil in the bowl of the oil burner and light it.

◆ Light the tea light (or votive) in the East, saying:
Air, breathe life.

◆ Light the tea light (or votive) in the South, saying:
Fire, ignite the spark.

◆ Light the tea light (or votive) in the West, saying:
Water, carry life.

◆ Light the tea light (or votive) in the North, saying:
Earth, deliver it.

◆ Light the green candle, saying to Demeter for her blessing:
Demeter, Goddess of the Corn
Bless me.

◆ Divide the corn into five equal bunches and, using the twine, bind it into the shape of a person. Use one bunch for its torso, with a head of corn at the top, and one bunch each for the arms and legs, as shown in the illustration on the right.

◆ As you are making your corn doll, mentally call the spirit of Demeter into it.

◆ Bind the green ribbon around the torso in criss-cross shapes, leaving sufficient ribbon to make a loop by which to hang it.

◆ Hang the corn doll on your bedpost, or above your bed, and remember to greet her each night before you retire.

Bedpost talisman spell

Increasing attractiveness

This spell is specifically for women who wish they were beautiful. Too good to be true? Not at all, but the principles involved do require you to rethink your concept of beauty. The fact is that each and every one of us is beautiful, but not every one of us has discovered it yet. This spell will help you find out how beautiful you are—and to flourish in that knowledge.

In a world where visual impact matters, women in particular are placed under a huge amount of pressure to look good. Very often the definition of what "good" is follows a line of fashion that demands that we alter our bodies in order to conform. At the moment the fashion is for thin women with flawless skins and do-as-it's-told hair, but no doubt this will change in time. For those of us who are built along more natural lines, with curves, birthmarks, and wild hair, beauty means discovering just how lovely we are.

We do not need to change our appearance to match what somebody else says is attractive, but we do need to appreciate our physical, mental, and spiritual selves more in order to bring out the best in us. This means learning to love ourselves for what we are, and lots of self-care so that those assets really shine! This is what makes us truly attractive to others.

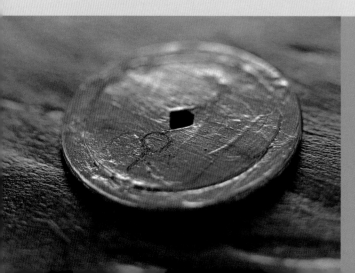

what you need...

One pink candle, approximately 6 inches/15 cm in length, placed in a secure holder • One pale green candle, approximately 6 inches/15 cm in length, placed in a secure holder • Geranium or jasmine incense, placed in a secure holder • Matches or a lighter • One masonry nail • One small copper disk with an eyelet (available from most craft stores) • 12 inches/30 cm of narrow red ribbon

what to do...

- Place the candles and incense safely on a surface within easy reach of your bed and light the incense.
- Seat yourself comfortably in the center of your bed, with the remaining ingredients in your lap. Close your eyes and concentrate on slowing your breathing, for 30 heartbeats.
- Visualize the space around your bed as a huge lake, with lotus flowers and petals floating on the surface, and relax as the ripples wash around you.
- Open your eyes and, keeping the vision of the lake in your head, light the pink candle, saying:
  I love myself.
- Light the green candle, saying:
  I am worthy of that love.
- Take the nail and, with the point, engrave on the copper disk the symbol of Venus, which is a circle with a cross attached to the bottom (see left).

- Pass the disk over the incense smoke, saying:
  I bless this talisman in the name of Aphrodite, goddess of love and attraction
  May it draw to me an understanding and appreciation of my own beauty.
- Holding the disk in your cupped hands, close your eyes and imagine yourself looking into the waters of the lake around the bed. Look at the reflection carefully before opening your eyes.
- Thread the narrow ribbon through the eyelet and secure the disk to your bedpost or above your bed.
- Repeat the visualization described above every time you feel unattractive or unloved, and practice the affirmations you made when you lit the candles as often as you need.
- Remember that you are beautiful.

Red candle spell

Attracting a new lover

This spell is intended for single people who are ready for a new lover to come into their lives. Since magic cannot interfere with the free will of another, or make someone love you, it is not aimed at attracting a particular person. Instead it asks for the right individual to come to you, once you decide the time is right for a new relationship. The wording of the spell specifies that the person should be worthy of you; this is to ensure that you don't end up with someone who is attracted to you, but has nothing else to recommend him or her as a future partner! Red is the color of love and passion, so make sure you use a red candle for this spell.

In classical mythology, Aphrodite, the Greek goddess of love, oversaw all aspects of romantic and sexual love. Legend tells us that she was born from the foam of the sea, connecting her to water, linked in magic to love and emotion. Known to the Romans as Venus, she has a planet named for her, sometimes known rather romantically as "The Evening Star" and a favorite for lovers to wish upon.

Friday is associated with the planet Venus, so this is the best day to put your love spell to the test. The correct moon phase for casting it is on a waxing moon.

what you need...

• Six drops of ylang-ylang, sandalwood, rose, or geranium essential oil • One red candle, approximately 6 inches/15 cm in length, placed in a secure holder
• One teaspoon of grapeseed, almond, or other carrier oil • Towel or tissue to wipe your hands on • Matches or a lighter

what to do...

- Immediately prior to this spell, take a bath, putting three drops of the essential oil into the hot water before you step in.
- Place the candle, in its holder, in the center of the room in which you will be working and position all the other items within easy reach.
- Sit on the floor in the center of the room, and visualize a circle of brilliant white light completely surrounding your work space. Say aloud:
  I call upon Aphrodite, goddess of beauty and love, to witness and aid me in this spell.
- When you are ready, put the remaining three drops of essential oil into the carrier oil.
- Take your candle in both hands and visualize a new lover coming toward you, smiling. Try not to focus on a particular person: let the features blur and change, as these are not important.
- Avoiding the wick, smear the oil over the candle using both hands, working from top to bottom, then bottom to top. Repeat these actions three times, then end by smearing from top to bottom. As you work, repeat aloud:
  Goddess of love, sweet Aphrodite,
  Send me a lover who's worthy of me.
- Wipe your hands on the towel or tissue, then light the candle, saying:
  Within three moons, so mote it be!
- When you are ready to leave your magical circle, place the candle somewhere safe and supervised while it burns down.

Candle-dipping spell

Making a wishing candle

The bedroom is a place for dreaming and also a place where wishes are born. It is often when we are dreaming, or just drifting into sleep, that our innermost desires appear to us. If these are worthy goals, there are ways in which we can work toward them, but a little magic is, of course, always useful.

In this spell you will be "enchanting" the candle as you make it, thus transferring the energy created by your chanting and wishing into the candle as you go along. When the candle is lit, the wish is released into the ether, where it will begin its work. Once you have acquired this method of "charging" an object with your

desires, you will be able to create spells of your own using it.

The technique of candle dipping is easy once you get the hang of it. It is best to remember to wipe away as much water as possible before dipping the candle back into the molten wax, as trapped water is the bane of hand-dipped tapers. Once you become more expert in this craft, you can add dye colors and appropriate essential oils to your repertoire.

Test this spell on a waxing moon, for wishing something to come toward you, or on a waning moon, if you are wishing something away. Any day of the week is suitable.

what you need...

One clean glass jar, with a minimum height of 6 inches/ 15 cm • One saucepan, with a minimum depth of 8 inches/20 cm • About 18 white household candles, approximately 6 inches/15 cm in length (the exact number depends on the circumference of your jar) • Some water • One jug, with a minimum height of 6 inches/15cm • One sheet of used newspaper • One metal skewer • One candle holder • One sheet of plain paper • 8 inches/20 cm of narrow blue ribbon

what to do...

◆ Place the jar in the center of the saucepan and fill it with as many candles as it will comfortably hold.

◆ Pour cold water into the saucepan all around the candle jar, to a level approximately 2 inches/5 cm below the lip, ensuring that the jar does not float.

◆ Place the saucepan and its contents onto a hot stove and heat the water to boiling point.

◆ Keeping the water bubbling, allow the wax in the jar to melt completely, placing new candles in it to melt down until the wax reaches about 1 inch/2.5 cm from the jar top.

◆ Fill the jug with cold water and place it on the newspaper next to the stove.

◆ Using the skewer, carefully fish out the wicks from the bottom of the jar. Pinch the top 1 inch/2.5 cm of wick between finger and thumb, and dip one wick in cold water, wipe off the water, then dip the wick into the wax.

◆ Repeat this process until the candle base is the right size to fit into your holder. Then allow the candle to cool, and roll it on the sheet of plain paper to smooth it.

◆ Boil up some water in a kettle to replace the water as it boils away in the pan.

◆ While undertaking this process, concentrate on your wish and send it into the candle by chanting:
Everything I change
Changes me
Everything changes
Endlessly.

◆ Tie the ribbon around the center of the candle and leave it under your pillow for six nights, burning it in your bedroom on the seventh.

BEDROOM SPELLS

Green Fairy spell

Keeping nightmares away

Children are sometimes troubled by bad dreams, for which a magical remedy can work wonders. The powers that you draw upon for this spell come from the kindness found within humans, and this is often personified, for children, by fairies. What better way than a pair of fairy wings to flap and drive away nightmares? This is a particularly fun spell and, with the parent's permission, the child concerned could benefit by participating in making other "Green Fairies" with you. With a little imagination, it should be possible to make a mobile, with a whole fleet of Green Fairy wings to flap away bad dreams should they come visiting.

Naturally the responsible adults in the child's life must ensure that nightmares are not occuring as a result of some terrible emotional turmoil such as bullying or abuse, and take any appropriate action. Encouraging the child to join in with making the fairy wings is quite therapeutic in itself, provided that the spell is carried out in conjunction with practical solutions. Children often have little rituals that they instinctively carry out when they feel troubled to create some protection around them. This can be very affirming and feel quite natural to them.

Use this spell on a New Moon or waning moon, to send away bad dreams, on any day of the week.

what you need...

Eight tea lights placed in secure holders or accompanied by a large heatproof mat • One green candle, approximately 6 inches/15 cm in length, placed in a secure holder • One frankincense or rosemary incense stick, placed in a secure holder • Matches or a lighter • One piece of 6 x 6 inch/15 x 15 cm green paper • One loaded office stapler • One 18 inch/45 cm length of pale or "invisible" thread • One tube of glitter glue, any color (available from craft stores)

what to do...

- Preferably, carry out this spell in the child's bedroom, with the child participating; otherwise, carry it out in your own bedroom.

- Gather all the ingredients in the center of the room, and place the tea lights in a "fairy ring," approximately 12 inches/30 cm in diameter.

- Place the green candle in its holder at the center, with the incense stick, and light all the surrounding tea lights.

- Light the green candle and the incense stick, saying:
  Spirit of kindness
  Lovely fairy
  Keep bad dreams at bay
  Send [my/child's name's] nightmares away.

- Take the green paper and fold it in an accordion shape, with folds at ½ inch/1 cm intervals.

- When it is completely folded, staple the paper "wings" at the center, using the stapler to secure the folds and fasten the end of the thread at the same time. You may need to staple twice for security.

- Open the fairy wings, which can be flattened out a little toward the center to form an open shape, and dab on some glitter.

- Help the glitter to dry by swinging the fairy wings in the air by the thread, and chant or sing the following rhyme:
  Stars and Moon come out to play
  [I am/child's name is] not afraid
  Nasty dreams have gone away
  Now [my/his/her] fairy's here to stay.

- Hang the Green Fairy wings above the child's bed or by the window, where the glitter may catch the light. Ensure that it is never hung near a naked flame or light bulb.

Clearing and Cleansing

Bathroom Spells

If the home is our sanctuary from the outside world, then the bathroom is

sometimes our refuge from the rest of our home. This is the space where we

cast off grime and anxiety, and recover our emotional and spiritual poise.

This chapter offers spells to regain a sense of balance, clear the mind, shed

bad habits, and wash the blues away.

BATHROOM SPELLS

Bath oil spell

Attaining inner harmony

The constant hustle and bustle of the modern world makes it particularly important that we find balance in our lives, because stress and anxiety can seriously compromise our health and general well-being. This touch of magic can ensure that any imbalance is redressed naturally and effectively.

There are a number of ways in which we can redress imbalances: by taking a serious look at our lifestyles and considering changes in our current lives. We might also consult alternative health practitioners, get some counseling, or take natural remedies. This spell combines a little magic with natural aromatherapy.

The oils used here have positive physiological effects as well as specific magical associations. Lavender is a favorite relaxant; it is magically linked with the element of Air, and has associations with mental stability. Geranium also has relaxing properties and often replaces the prohibitively expensive rose absolute oil. Bergamot, used to lift the spirits, is magically linked to the Sun, and is employed to help you to "recharge" your energies.

Perform this spell over three consecutive evenings. Use it whenever you need it, at any phase of the moon, and on any day of the week, for the moon's cycle itself is a form of continual balance.

what you need...

One clean pipette (fine glass tube), thin spatula, or drinking straw • 2 teaspoons/10 ml almond carrier oil • One clean, empty essential-oil bottle • Nine drops each of lavender, geranium, and bergamot essential oils • One standard sewing needle • Three tea lights (or votives) • One glass tea light holder • Matches or a lighter

what to do...

- Gather all the ingredients in your bathroom, run a bath for yourself, and slip into a bathrobe.
- Using the pipette, spatula, or drinking straw, place the almond carrier oil in the empty bottle.
- Place three drops of lavender essential oil into the bottle, saying:
  Lavender for rest and growth
  As I bathe, help me do both.
- Add another three drops, saying:
  Three by two
  May each come true.
- Then add the last three drops, saying:
  Three by three
  So mote it be!
- Repeat this process with the geranium and bergamot essential oils in turn, using the same words for the second and third set of drops as above, but substituting the following words for the first drops, as appropriate:

Geranium to love myself
Geranium to balance health.
Bergamot for energy
Herb of the sun, shine bright in me.

- Stir the mixture thoroughly.
- Slip off your robe and, with the point of the needle, inscribe in the surface of one tea light (or votive) your initial and the symbol of the Sun, which is a circle with a dot in the center.
- Set this in a glass holder, and place it by the side of the bath. Light it, step into the bath, and soak in the essentail oil mixture, allowing your mind to float free of everyday worries.
- Allow the tea light (or votive) to burn down completely, and repeat the whole process on the following two nights.
- If you apply this spell at regular intervals, you will find your own inner balance.

Power shower spell

Clearing your mind

Although this spell is ideally suited to people who have busy or stressful lives, it can be used by anyone who wants to free his or her mind of clutter. It works as a powerful combination of the acts of physical and psychological cleansing. The spell also stimulates the energy points in your body, which will keep you protected from the mental and physical stress that can accumulate during the day. And it applies whether you go out to work or stay at home.

The spell is suitable for a morning or evening shower, and can be repeated as many times as you wish. If you do not have a shower, you can easily adapt it for use in the bath: simply take a clean, empty dishwashing-liquid bottle, and in your bath squirt clean water onto the appropriate energy points. The purpose of this action is to strengthen those energy points most likely to be affected by daily stress, and which, if invigorated, are most likely to guard you from it.

This spell can be used in any moon phase because it both cleanses and strengthens your mind. Any day of the week can be stressful, depending on your circumstances and lifestyle, so it is not restricted to a particular day or time. Just enjoy this cleansing process whenever you feel in need!

what you need...

Three drops each of pine and juniper essential oil • One handful of dry, large flaked oatmeal • 12 mint leaves • One mixing bowl and spoon • One clean 6 x 6 inch/15 x 15 cm piece of muslin or other open-weave cloth • One 8 inch/20 cm length of string or ribbon

what to do...

- Stir the essential oils, oatmeal, and mint together in the mixing bowl, using the spoon.
- Place the mixture in the center of the muslin square, gather up the corners, and tie the string or ribbon around the top, making sure it is long enough to hang over a shower head (or bath tap).
- Once you are in the shower, rub the sachet over your body until you feel fresh and clean.
- As the water runs over you, visualize all your mental clutter, stress, and anxieties being washed away while you chant.
- If you are taking a shower in the evening, chant:
  Troubles of the day;
  Wash them all away.
- If you are taking a shower in the morning, chant:
  Cobwebs of the night;
  Put them all to flight.
- When you feel completely cleansed, turn the shower pressure to maximum, then direct the jet toward the center of your abdomen, visualizing the energy point there as a ball of yellow light.
- Next, direct it toward your chest at heart level, visualizing the energy point there as a ball of green light.
- Step out of the shower and dry yourself, while visualizing a shield of protection emanating from your energy points.

Cactus spell

Shedding unhealthy habits

Because the bathroom is a place where we cast off dirt and grime, it is also an ideal space in which to base magical spells for ridding ourselves of things we no longer want or need, and for starting afresh. This spell is designed to shed bad habits and fend off their return. It uses a cactus plant, for which a well-lit bathroom is the ideal indoor habitat.

Not all habits are harmful, but many—such as smoking, starving and binging, substance abuse, and some behavioral traits—are downright unhealthy. If these are seriously affecting your life, you may need to seek advice from an appropriate support group. Such habits are often

symptoms of other problems in our lives that need exploring and resolving. However, the habit itself causes its own damage, and this spell can be a reinforcement for your recovery; declaring your determination to cast off damaging behavior can be extremely self- and life-affirming.

Other habits such as nail biting, knuckle cracking, or chewing gum may seem petty compared to more serious problems, but if it is irritating you (and others around you), then they are still worthy of this magical treatment.

Cast this spell on a waning moon to dispel your habit, and on a Tuesday to give you the willpower and courage to banish it.

what you need...

One tea light (or votive), placed in a secure holder
• Matches or a lighter • Nine sewing needles
• Tweezers or scissors • One green candle, cut to approximately 4–5 inches/10–13 cm in length, placed in a secure holder • One small screwtop jar • One potted spiky cactus • A little water

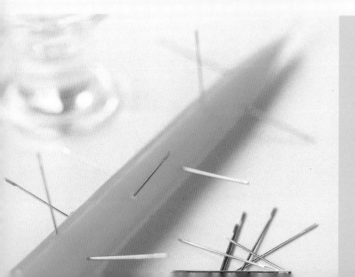

what to do...

- Gather all the ingredients together in the bathroom.
- Light the tea light (or votive) and, holding a needle at the eye end with tweezers or scissors, put the pointed end in the flame until it glows red hot.
- Push half the needle, point first, horizontally into the green candle.
- Repeat this process with the remaining eight needles, sticking them at different points along the candle's length, so that it eventually has nine needles sticking out of it.
- Hold the base of the candle in both hands and, concentrating hard on the habit you wish to shed, say:
  As these nine needles fall,
  My [habit] will fall away.
  As these nine needles drop,
  My [habit] will be discarded.
- When you are ready to let go of the habit, light the candle, and watch as the first needles drop.
- When the candle has completely burned down, remove all the needles, place them in the jar, and screw the top on firmly, saying:
  You have been burned,
  Never return.
- Bury the jar in your garden away from the house, where it will be undisturbed.
- Place the cactus in your bathroom, saying:
  Defend me from [habit]
  Good friend.
- Water the cactus sparingly, and keep it in your bathroom.
- Visualize a new, positive habit to replace the one you have just shed and to ensure that the bad habit does not return—and act on it!

Soap spell

Washing the blues away

Imagine coming home after a long, hard day, or getting the children to bed at last, and wishing you could just wash all your tiredness and worries away. This spell is designed to do exactly that—so if you have ever wished you could wash the day away, read on! It requires a little prior preparation, but is well worth the effort. Collect remnants of used soap to recycle as a modern-day "witch ball," or an object in which power is contained. You will need to soak them for a day or two, so that they are nicely soft when you come to make your soap ball. This should be kept separately from the communal toiletries because it is for your use only.

In this spell you are employing magic to symbolically wash away your cares, so you will be using a magically charged soap. As you wash, visualize the worries that "cling" to you as having a physical presence, so that the act of washing translates into ridding yourself of the anxiety that has built up during the day. This form of visualization can be highly therapeutic and empowering in its own right; teamed with a little magical knowhow, it is doubly effective!

Make the soap ball on a waning moon, to carry your troubles away, and preferably on Saturday, the day of Saturn the banisher; but use it at the end of any day when you feel weary.

what you need...

Sufficient remnants of soap to make a soap ball 2–3 inches/ 5–7.5 cm in diameter • One bowl • A little warm water • One black candle, approximately 6 inches/15 cm in length, placed in a secure holder • Matches or a lighter • Nine leaves of fresh mint, chopped • Three drops of rosemary essential oil • One white tea light (or votive), placed in a secure holder

what to do...

- Place the slivers of soap in the bowl and cover them with a little warm water. Leave them to soak for a day or two until they are soft and pliable, then drain off the water.
- The next night take all the ingredients to the bathroom and place the bowl of soap remnants in the sink.
- Light the candle, saying:
  Strong Saturn the banisher
  Pour your energy into this spell
  To wash away worries
  That all will be well.
- Place the chopped mint and rosemary essential oil in the bowl with the soap.
- Knead the soap, blending in the mint and oil, and adding a little warm water if necessary to keep the soap soft. As you do this, chant:
  I cast in the power
  To wash and to scour.
- Form the mixture into a ball, and leave it to dry undisturbed in front of the candle.
- When you need to wash the cares of the day away, light a tea light (or votive), climb into the shower, and use your soap "witch ball," visualizing your anxieties being washed away as described on page 110.
- As you wash yourself down, banish your worries by singing a favorite song, or by chanting the following words:
  Worries on me and round about
  I throw you off and cast you out.

Going Outside

Backdoor and garden spells

The outer boundaries of our home represent mental and emotional as well

as physical markers of our personal space, and their importance should

never be underestimated. This final chapter contains spells to keep your

space secure and protected, nourish your garden, plant wishes, keep

away unwanted visitors, and ensure that the outside world keeps in

touch when you need it to.

Scarecrow spell

Securing and protecting your home

There are many ancient traditions relating to guarding the home from intruders: magic has been used to keep unwanted visitors away for thousands of years. Archeologists have discovered amulets, magical symbols, and even curses to keep strangers away from homes, temples, and tombs all over the world, in many cultures dating from various periods. This spell is an up-to-date version of an ancient tradition of keeping unwelcome people away from your home.

Our homes are perhaps the most intimate spaces that we inhabit, so they merit special consideration when it comes to whom we invite in—and whom we keep out. Many people claim that the feeling of personal invasion when a burglary occurs is much stronger than the feeling of loss attached to the stolen property.

This spell sets up a magical guardian at the back of your home, in the shape of a scarecrow. Prior to spell casting, you need to think of a name for it: your guardian can be male, female, or neither, and you will need to treat it respectfully once the spell is cast. Do not reveal its name to any other person. Lollipop sticks or craft store wood can be used to make the pole and crosspiece. Cast the spell on a New Moon, which is best for protective magic—if this falls on a Saturday, then so much the better.

what you need...

One black candle, approximately 6 inches/15 cm in length, placed in a secure holder • Matches or a lighter • Craft tape • A wooden center pole, approximately 12 inches/30 cm high • A wooden crosspiece, approximately 8 inches/20 cm long • One ball of twine • Four knitted-cotton dishtowels • One sewing needle and thread • Two large buttons • One fiber-tipped marker pen • One old baby jacket or sweater • One old hat

what to do...

- Gather all the ingredients together in any room of the house.
- Light the candle and work silently.
- Tape the center pole and crosspiece together, about 3 inches/7.5 cm from the top of the center pole, and secure firmly with twine.
- Roll three dishtowels together into a ball, cover with the fourth, and sew firmly in place to form the head.
- Sew on buttons as eyes, and use the marker pen to draw a nose and an X where the mouth should be.
- Clothe the scarecrow, using the baby jacket or sweater and old hat.
- Hold your guardian up in front of the candle, and say:
  I name you [name]
  I name you Guardian of my home
  I name you Protector of its boundaries
  I empower you to turn back intruders
  I will this by sea and sky,
  I will it by field and flame
  So mote it be!
- Position your guardian in a flowerpot or in the earth, facing outward toward the rear of your property, where he or she can best guard it.

New Moon spell

Helping your garden grow

Whether you have a windowbox or manage large, sweeping grounds, you will understand the importance of placating the spirit of the garden. Ensuring that your best-laid plans and hard work all come to fruition is the aim of this spell, and it is based on an ancient tradition.

Nowadays, the wisdom of working with the Earth and with nature is becoming more obvious to us. Ancient peoples, who lived more in tandem with the cycle of the seasons, recognized the importance of giving back what you took from the soil. In some parts of the world the custom of leaving a gift in the soil when you

take a plant or lop a branch from a tree is still followed. This spell creates an offering for the Earth to ensure fertility and growth, and to ask for a blessing for your garden and all that grows there. This practice will create a special bond between you and your garden, and will ensure a fine crop of flowers and vegetables for the coming season.

Carry out this spell at the New Moon, when the Moon's disk is entirely overshadowed and no part of it appears in the sky; this is sometimes called "Dark Moon" by witches, for that very reason. Traditionally, farmers plant seeds at the New Moon for the best chance of success, so this is a good time to "plant" your offering.

what you need...

One green candle, either a tea light (votive) or a candle cut to approximately 3 inches/7.5 cm in length, placed in a secure holder • One clean jar 5–6 inches/13–15 cm high • Matches or a lighter • One dessertspoon • One glass of red wine (or grape juice, if you are avoiding alcohol) • ½ oz/15 g bread, taken from the center of the loaf • One gold- or bronze-colored coin, any denomination • One teaspoon of clear honey • One garden trowel

what to do...

- After dark, at the New Moon, go out into your garden, taking all the ingredients with you.
- Place the candle inside the jar to guard the flame from the wind, and light it, saying:
  I dedicate this flame to the spirit of the Earth.
- Pour a dessertspoon measure of the red wine onto the bread.
- Press the coin into the center of the bread.
- Spread the bread with honey.
- In the center of your garden, using the trowel, dig a small hole about 6 inches/15 cm deep, and place the wine-and-honey-soaked bread and coin at the bottom of it.

- Place your hand palm down over the hole, saying:
  To this Earth I give the blessings of wealth, wholeness, sweetness, and nourishment
  May this good Earth return the same to me.
- Cover the offering and fill in the hole with the soil originally dug from it, leveling it off appropriately.
- Drink a toast to the spirit of the Earth with the red wine, pouring a little onto the ground before you finish the glass.
- Allow the candle to burn down completely, under supervision.

BACKDOOR AND
GARDEN SPELLS

Daffodil spell

Growing wishes

Growing plants helps us to create beautiful homes and to mark the boundaries of our property. If you don't have a backyard or garden, you could always create a windowbox with colorful flowers instead. Using a flower bulb in magic is very appropriate. Spells can be regarded as the bulb or seed of something that we want to make happen in our lives: we plant spells like bulbs and hope they will grow. Here, the daffodil bulb is used to symbolize and contain your wish, and as the plant grows and flourishes, whatever you have wished for will eventually come to you.

Spells generally succeed when we ask for things that are really needed, rather than something that might just be a passing fancy. Whatever you ask for, remember that magic works with—not against—nature, so use your spells for need rather than greed. Remember to keep your wish simple, and concentrate on the desired outcome rather than the means by which it will come about. Entrust that part to the spell for maximum success.

Try out this spell on a waxing moon, for growth and attraction. Any day of the week is suitable, except Saturday, which is the day of restrictive Saturn and should be avoided.

what you need...

One yellow candle, approximately 6 inches/15 cm in length, placed in a secure holder • Three sheets of old newspaper • Matches or a lighter • One small gardening trowel or dessertspoon • Bulb compost to fill the pot • One standard plant pot, approximately 5 inches/13 cm in diameter • One standard daffodil bulb

what to do...

- Place the candle, in its holder, in the center of the room in which you will be working and put the newspaper on the floor within easy reach. Place all the other items on the newspaper.
- Sitting in the center of the room, visualize a circle of golden light completely surrounding the space in which you will be working.
- Light the candle, saying:
  I call upon Air to carry my spell,
  I call upon Fire to warm it,
  I call upon Water to feed it,
  I call upon Earth to nourish it,
  I call upon Spirit to bless it.
- Using the trowel or spoon, put compost into the plant pot until it is half full, then take the bulb in both hands and concentrate on your wish.
- Still holding the bulb, close your eyes and visualize whatever you are wishing for actually happening.

- Open your eyes and, looking and speaking directly to the flower bulb, say:
  By this spell and by my will,
  May my wishes be fulfilled.
- Breathe in deeply, and direct your breath onto the bulb, willing your wish into it.
- Plant the bulb, roots down, in the potting compost, adding more until the top of the bulb is covered by about ½ inch/1 cm of compost.
- Place the pot in a dark, dry cupboard until the shoot is approximately 2½ inches/6 cm high, then bring it into the daylight. Either transplant the bulb to your backyard, garden, or windowbox, or keep it indoors in the original pot.
- It is important to care for your plant as enthusiastically as you care about your wish. Follow the instructions on the bulb package, and enjoy watching your flower grow and bloom, for only then will your wish come true.

Ringstone spell

Guarding the home from unwanted visitors

When you are at home you can't always keep the world away, but it is good to be able to ward off unwelcome or wearisome visitors who tend to "drop in" without warning. This spell offers some protection from those guests whom you would rather didn't drop in unannounced!

In magical tradition a "ringstone," sometimes called a "hagstone," has a hole worn through it naturally by the sea and is thought to offer powerful protection to the wearer. Such stones are quite rare and are highly valued in the occult community. Today it is possible to buy inexpensive "donut" stones from "New Age"

outlets or gift stores. If you can't track one down, you can make your own from fast-drying modeling clay. You simply need to prepare it a bit ahead of time. If you use clay, remember to seal it and make it waterproof with varnish, as the ringstone will hang outside and will need to be suitable for all weather conditions.

A ringstone nailed to the front gate or doorpost will send out a magical signal that not everyone is always welcome to drop in unannounced. Don't worry that it will be forbidding to everyone—it will not keep away good friends or thoughtful relatives. Cast this spell on a waning moon, and if possible, on Saturday, the day of the ringed planet Saturn.

what you need...

One ringstone, as described above • One white candle, approximately 6 inches/15cm in length, placed in a secure holder • One black candle, approximately 6 inches/15 cm in length, placed in a secure holder • Matches or a lighter • One salt shaker filled with salt, with a single hole for pouring • One 6–8 inch/15–20 cm length of strong, narrow cord • Hammer • One nail

what to do...

- Gather all the ingredients in the center of the room in which you will be working, using the table or floor to lay out the items.

- Place the ringstone in the center of your work space, with the white candle to the right and the black candle to the left.

- Visualizing a bright white circle encompassing the entire house, light the white candle, saying:

  This house is favored by the light brought into
  It by good company.

- Light the black candle, saying:

  This house is protected by the light brought to
  Defend it from unwelcome company.

- Pour a circle of salt all around the ringstone, saying:

  Pure salt, protect and circle round
  And bless this home as sacred ground
  That I/we may live in peace
  And from poor company be released.

- Pick up the ringstone, blow away the salt circle, and take the stone, cord, hammer, and nail immediately to your front gate or door.

- Thread the cord through the stone and tie it firmly. Hammer the nail into the gate or post, and hang the stone by the cord to keep those unwanted visitors at bay.

BACKDOOR AND GARDEN SPELLS

Mailbox spell

Ensuring the flow of communication to your home

Most households benefit from an easy flow of communication within the home, but sociability and good company are assured by the clear flow of communication into the home from outside. This spell encourages connections with friends and welcome elements of your family.

Naturally, to keep communications going, you need to respond to letters, e-mails, and telephone calls as they come, but this spell is great for initiating new links and maintaining old connections. It uses the principle of sympathetic magic—and the mail—to encourage friends, relatives, and even new acquaintances to make contact.

It has often been observed that happy households are generally those that stay busy in terms of visits, invitations, and activities that are planned and arranged within them. This spell attracts social and family connections to your door, so if you would like to have that choice, cast away and put this spell to the test! Be assured that casting it doesn't mean that you will be hosting a party every other evening— unless you want to! It simply draws welcome contact toward you.

Cast this spell on a waxing moon, to draw letters, e-mails, telephone calls, and welcome visitors to your home, and on a Wednesday, the day of the communication's planet Mercury.

what you need...

One standard sewing needle • One tea light (or votive) • Matches or a lighter • One piece of 8¼ x 11⅝ inches/A4 paper • One pen • One pale gray or white bird feather, shed naturally • One plain 8¼ x 11⅝ inches/A4 envelope • One postage stamp

what to do...

- Assemble all the ingredients in your hallway, if possible, or in the room in which you will be working.
- Using the point of the needle, inscribe into the surface of a tea light (or votive) the symbol of Mercury, which is a circle with a cross attached at the bottom and an upward-pointing arc at the top.
- Light the tea light (or votive), saying:
  Mercury, patron of communication
  Witness and bless this spell.
- In the center of the paper, draw a horizontal line with an arrow at each end, pointing in opposite directions. Above this, draw the symbol for Mercury again.
- Place the feather in the center of the paper, and fold the paper up to fit into the envelope.

- Place them inside the envelope and seal it.
- Address the envelope to your home and put the stamp on it.
- Hold it up in front of the tea light (or votive), and say the following words:
  Fly through the ether
  Swift and sure
  Carry good company
  Here to my door.
- Close your eyes and visualize letters being delivered through the mailbox, and see yourself answering welcome telephone calls and receiving interesting e-mails.
- Mail the letter as soon as possible, then stock up on cookies, tea, and coffee for visitors!

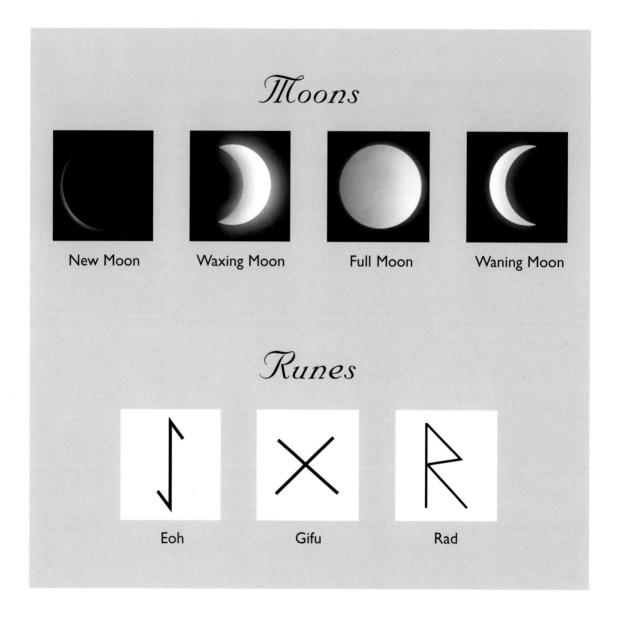

Moons

New Moon   Waxing Moon   Full Moon   Waning Moon

Runes

Eoh   Gifu   Rad

The publisher wishes to thank the following for supplying the pictures in this book:

p 13 Alan Weintraub/Arcaid (top right); ©Philippa Lewis; Eddifice/Corbis (top left); ©Steve Raymer/Corbis (bottom left); ©Jeremy Homer/Corbis (bottom right)

p 20 Chris Craymer/Getty Images (bottom)

p 43 Uwe Krejci/Getty Images

p 44 ©Dennis Cicco/Corbis (top)

p 49 ©Tania Midgley/Corbis

p 52 ©Richard T Nowitz/Corbis (bottom)

p 56 Rob Melnychuk/Getty Images (bottom)

p 57 ©Laura Doss/Corbis

p 69 ©Rob Melnychuk/Corbis

p 71 ©Lito C. Uyan/Corbis

p 73 Cesar Lucas Abreu/Getty

p 75 ©David Muench/Corbis

p 81 © Angela H/Bubbles Photo Library

p 87 ©Clay Perry/Corbis

p 91 ©Eric Henderson/Corbis

p 95 Willie Maldonado/Getty

p 96 ©Rob Lewine/Corbisstockmarket.com

p 98 ©Dennis Cicco/Corbis (top)

p 101 Jennie Woodcock ; Reflections Photolibrary/Corbis

p 117 ©Michael Boys/Corbis

p 123 Ryan McVay/Getty